I REMAIN,
YOUR SON JACK
– Letters from
The First World War

J.C. Morten

Edited by Sheila Morten

Published by Sigma Leisure – an imprint of
Sigma Press, 1 South Oak Lane, Wilmslow, Cheshire SK9 6AR, England.

Whilst every effort has been made to ensure that the information given in this book is correct, neither the publisher nor the author accept any responsibility for any inaccuracy.

British Library Cataloguing in Publication Data

A CIP record for this book is available from the British Library.

ISBN: 1-85058-346-3

Typesetting and Design by: Sigma Press, Wilmslow, Cheshire. For the technically minded: the letters were word-processed with Microsoft Word on an Apple Macintosh and then converted to MS-DOS format prior to final setting and layout.

Cover design and illustration: Colin Curbishley

Printed by : Manchester Free Press, Paragon Mill, Jersey Street, Manchester M4 6FP

Foreword

Much of the strength of the British military system has been the establishing of regimental roots deep into the cities and countryside in the form of the Volunteer movement. This has created a unique esprit de corps which exists in no other army in the world.

7th Battalion The Manchester Regiment, which the young Jack Morten had joined, traces its own roots back to 1859 when it began life as the 40th Lancashire Rifle Volunteers or 3rd Manchester. In 1880 its title was changed to the 16th Lancashire Rifle Volunteers and the following year the battalion became an integral part of The Manchester Regiment. In 1888 it was designated as the 4th Volunteer Battalion The Manchester Regiment and in 1908, as a result of the Haldane reforms, was designated the 7th Battalion The Manchester Regiment (Territorial Force).

The 7th Manchesters mobilised at their Burlington Street Headquarters on 4th August 1914 and five weeks later embarked for Egypt as part of the 42nd (East Lancashire) Division. The letters which form this book, of a young Territorial later to be commissioned into his own battalion, provide a fascinating account of his thoughts and experiences, often written under the most miserable conditions before and after the heat of battle.

Sheila Morten is to be congratulated, not only on rescuing and publishing these letters, but also on the painstaking research which she has carried out into the activities of the battalion in which her father-in-law served and fought. It is an important addition to the published histories of The Manchester Regiment.

Captain R.A. Bonner

Chairman, The Manchester Museum Committee of The King's Regiment – 'Museum of The Manchesters'

. . . in a shoe box hidden on the floor . .

Preface

John Clarke Morten was born on 24th January 1892, the son of a manufacturer's agent who marketed stiff collars and who was also a pillar of Mount Tabor Methodist Church in Stockport. He was educated at Stockport Grammar School, then joined his father at his office in Manchester. He was a lacrosse player with the Heaton Mersey Club and enlisted in 1914, along with many lacrosse players from the area, in the Manchester Regiment, serving with the 1st/7th (Territorial) Battalion. After the war he joined forces with Thomas Hardman and Company who made felts for the papermaking trade and was a representative for them until his death in 1948. In 1925 he married Phyllis Nield who died in 1986. They had one son, Denys.

These letters turned up in a shoe box hidden on the floor at the back of his widow's garage when it was cleared out in the early months of 1987. They were neatly tied with string, ribbon or wool and several contained photographs with captions written on the back. Everything was as fresh as a daisy. Alongside was a bag containing exercise books in which Jack Morten's mother had copied each of the letters as she received them. Nothing had been said about them in recent years, though my husband had been told, some time ago, of their existence (though not their whereabouts!) We were captivated on settling down to read such a delightful collection of letters and it gives us great pleasure to share them with you, the reader.

Many people helped with the gathering of information to substantiate the events mentioned in the letters. I received particulat help from: R.D. Morten; Stalybridge Library; The Museum of the Manchesters, Ashton Town Hall; Central Library, Manchester; Stockport Library; the immediate past occupants of Arnwood; Pam Malobon; Pat Hardman; G.B. Saunders; Don Ibbotson, who made prints of the photographs; people in and around Cloughton; The Imperial War Museum.

Sheila Morten

J.C. (Jack) Morten

Contents

LETTERS AND SHOE-BOXES

It's strange how old letters are often discovered in shoe-boxes, but this is how this collection came to light. Before we begin with the letters themselves, on these first two pages is the ubiquitous box, one of the letters sent by Jack (with an envelope addressed to his mother) and a close-up of his signature. The rest, as they say, is history and a fascinating collection of personal anecdotes.

*Above: 'Arnwood',
destination of the letters.*

*Right: the shoe-box, packed
tightly with the letters*

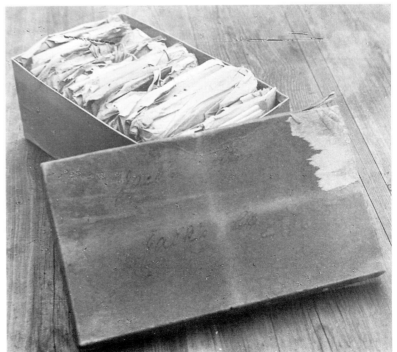

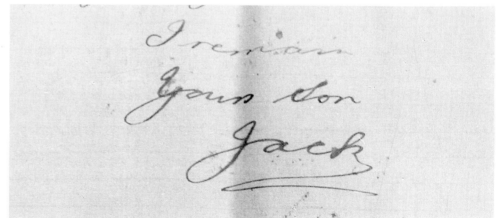

One of Jack's letters and, below, how he signed off.

ARRIVAL AT LITTLEBOROUGH AND JOURNEY TO SOUTHAMPTON

READY,
AYE
READY!

FOR DEFENCE OF
HEARTH AND HOME.

Postcard
Sept 4 1914

We have arrived at Littleborough[†] & may be leaving anytime, so come as soon as you can. Having a jolly good rough & tumble time.

Yours, love
Jack

Hollingworth Camp
Littleborough
Sept 6 1914

Dear Mother,

We haven't gone yet, although we've packed up about ten times & labelled our packs & guns, they are fairly mugging us about. When you come over next time, will you bring me my swimming costume, white sweater & lacrosse trousers. This life is absolutely ideal. Every morning we are up at 5 o'clock & go for Swedish drill[‡], running & swimming, then we go back for breakfast about 9 o'clock, & after that we go for a march with full kit on, come back perspiring like rabbits, because when our full kit is on we are carrying between 80 & 90 lbs, so you can tell, after a few miles march with drill at the end of it one feels pretty well done up.

I'm glad to say that after noon we do no work at all except our private business such as mending socks & washing shirts, so taking things all round I'm having a ripping time. This afternoon I've been stitching buttons on my tunic, then afterwards about twenty of us went for a session with Major Staveacre & Captain Smedley, & about ten of us swam the width of the lake, not a bad swim – it's equal to 500 yards & it was tip-top.

---

†Littleborough is near Rochdale in Lancashire.
‡Swedish Drill - physical jerks, mostly on the spot.
§His sister, Martha Annes, usually called Pat, Patty or Pattie.

Well Mother, I must close now. Give my love to Father, Patty§ & Pauline (the Welsh girl). Hoping to see you soon.

I remain
With love

Jack
Sept 9 1914

We are off at last & our company is guarding the Station†. It will be great sport standing there keeping the crowd back whilst the other companies enter, then we ourselves go to Southampton tonight. Last night, after I left you we met Miss Marshall & Co & what do you think, Mrs Broadhurst kissed me & wished me luck, after not looking at me for two years. I cannot give you my address now, as I don't quite know but I will let you have it as soon as possible. Well, Mother dear, I haven't the time to write more now as I can hear the Sergeant calling our Company to fall in. Remember me to everybody & give my love to Father. I'll write as soon as I can & I'm as happy as a King, so don't worry.

Yours with love

Jack

PS I think it's Egypt we are going to, if not there it will be Cyprus.

Postcard
Sept 10 1914

We are now on the boat at Southampton after having had a fine train ride. They were very short of room so four of us were put in a first class compartment & we travelled like lords the whole of the way. I'll write as soon as possible.

---

†The Battalion left Littleborough just after midnight on 10 September 1914 as part of the East Lancashire Division Territorials. There were 598 Officers and 18077 Men. They took 5600 horses, 38 x 15 pounders, 12 Howitzers, 24 Machine Guns, 239 carts, 400 wagons and "an enormous quantity of luggage". It must have been quite a sight!

VOYAGE ON THE
GRANTULLY CASTLE†

Sept 15 1914

I am now safely on the way & roughing it like an old Tar. We left Southampton on Thursday 10th & have not yet reached Gibraltar, terribly slow isn't it? but you see there are 15 ships all sailing together, amongst them being 2 Cruisers. I can tell you, it's a jolly fine sight in mid ocean seeing so many together, & it's a coincidence that might never happen again. It took us two days to cross the Bay of Biscay & I can't really explain to you what we went through, as of course, like all troop ships we are fairly crowded, & for sleeping we have the same room as we mess in.

Every night about 8.30 we all go down & sling our hammocks, & when they are slung you couldn't put a pin between them, so you can understand what it was like crossing the Bay with one half of the men sick. I'm very fortunate as the first night we slung them each of us rushed for a spot to sling them, & that place we put our names on the rafters overhead & naturally for the rest of the voyage we have to stick to that particular place. Well I looked round & slung mine just at the bottom of the hatch & the whole night through there is a nice draught, & on each side of me there is Bert Smith & Frank Lomas, so I know who my next neighbours are.

I hope you will be able to decipher this, but I am writing under difficulties, namely in semi-darkness as there are some bally pie-cans‡ who keep walking past in front of the port-holes. It was so beastly & stuffy on Sunday night, & we had not got through the Bay, that Harry & myself took our blanket & slept up on the deck. It was most Bohemian as we had to slip past the guard & kind of smuggle ourselves in a corner. It was most funny: Powell thought he would do the same thing and lay down about five yards from us, but was not quite so discreet, so when the guard walked round about 4 o'clock in the morning poor old Powell was fired off to his bunk, & Harry & myself lay there quite unnoticed & it was jolly fine. There was a starry sky & all around us the waves of the deep blue sea lulling one to sleep, but I mustn't get poetical or I might do Bill Shakespeare out of a job.

We have now passed Cape Finnisterre & there is a wonderful change in the weather, so tropical that they are now preparing the decks so that all the hammocks can be slung at night

---

†The Grantully Castle sailed from Southampton on 10 September 1914 with a convoy of 14 ships plus one ammunition ship with 7 million rounds on board, escorted by HMS Minerva. They were the first Territorial Division to leave England on Active Service.
‡Piecans - idiots

on deck, instead of in the stuffy mess-room. Last night more than one half of the troops on board slept on deck including the Stockport contingent, & I am now writing on the floor of the deck in the broiling hot sun, just recovering from a meal, the first I have had since I came on board, as I lived on apples for two days, which I bought from the dry canteen.

This life is really an ideal lazy one; it's now Tuesday & I've done the first bit of work this morning since I came on board. We were lined up on deck for Swedish drill & the Sergeant came & asked for six men, so Baty & myself offered ourselves as there was work to be done, & we had the job of swabbing the decks & stairs down the hatch. I can tell you I'm getting quite domesticated, & when I come home, I'll have a competition with Father & Tom at carving.

On the Grantully Castle. JCM is bottom left

It is now Wednesday & we have just passed Cape St. Vincent so we are only 170 miles from Gibraltar which we hope to pass tonight. I'm rather sorry that we are not passing it in the daytime as I should like to have had a look at the old Rock, but I shall have a good view if the night is clear & starry as I'm on guard today. I have to keep the door of the wash-house & see that too many don't go & wash at once, or else the place would get crowded. It's a fine job as nobody can have a wash until they first of all ask me if they can. I'm on this duty for 24 hours. I started at 10 o'clock a.m. for two hours then I am on again at 10 o'clock p.m. for another two hrs, and my last shift is in the morning from *4a.m.* till 6 a.m..

This morning we passed several whales, they were like young elephants swimming about. You might remember me to all my pals & tell Aunt Alice that I have already filled about six pages of the diary which she sent me. Of course when I get to Khartum & fairly settled in barracks I will send them a letter, but I can't write to everybody on this tub as the only writing tables we have is the floor of the boat, so you can understand under such conditions writing becomes a nuisance.

I hope this letter will reach you, but up to now I haven't been able to get a stamp anywhere & there are none to be bought on board. Give my best wishes to Tom & tell him to keep his pecker up, & tell him there are several Port Erin[†] boys on board. Remember me to Father, Pat & Lena[‡]. Tell Father I should like to know how things are at the Office. You can write to

Private Morten
No 2393
D Company
7th Manchesters
Egypt

So far this is the only address I can give you.

With best Love

I remain
Your Son
Jack

Wednesday Sept 23 1914

I haven't really much to write about as we see nothing all day but water, but I thought that I would let you know that I'm still living & having a good time in one sense, as it's an absolute change from my normal routine. We passed Malta[§] on Sunday & there was a

[†]Port Erin - Isle of Man.
[‡]Lena - The Housekeeper who remained with the family until the 1940's.
[§]Malta was passed on 21st September, and they arrived in Alexandria on 25th September. Arriving in Port Sudan on 30th September, they then travelled by train from Atbara to Khartoum arriving on 2nd October to a temperature of 105 degrees.

rumour that we were calling there, but I'm sorry to say that we did not. We kept stopping near there & afterwards we heard that one of the Cruisers had captured a German liner.

I was inoculated last Thursday & the same day I was put on guard for 24 hours. I was done in my arm as I thought it would be stronger than my chest & therefore less likely to take bad ways. Of course, for 48 hrs my arm was very sore, but now I have the use of it & feel in the pink.

I had a very busy day on Monday – I washed my shirt & several towels & I'm hanged if the best laundry in England could have done them better under such conditions, as we had nothing but salt water & I couldn't get a lather; of course the things weren't what you would call spotless, but they were a little bit fresher. This voyage is teaching one self denial, as you can't buy scarcely a thing on board. If I hadn't brought this writing pad with me I & a few others would have been in a hopeless mess. The only cigarettes we can buy are Woodbines & the only tobacco, a kind of twist. Even the matches now are at a premium & you can't get any for love or money. I've got about half a box left & I prize them like quids.

The food is not quite as plentiful as it was in camp & not so good, as we have no variety. Every morning we get porridge without milk, sugar or syrup, so we usually spread jam on it, as jam is one of the few luxuries we can buy. For dinner we have meat which can't always be named with jacket potatoes, & twice a week pudding, either plum duff or rice which I relish as though it were bit of turkey (I'm always hungry).

I will now tell you of a piece of luck which has come my way. I've got to know one of the stewards in the pantry & I go down there twice a day & have a ripping meal & coffee every night. Of course I have to keep it very quiet & can't even take one of my pals as there is one little corner of the pantry into which I go & have all sorts of tasty bits such as liver & bacon, asparagus, chicken etc, the same food that the officers have, & all this I get for a cigar or cigarette.

Every morning I have a sea-water bath on board about 5 o'clock just to make me feel fit for breakfast which is 6.30 a.m. Then we lounge about until Swedish drill which is about 9.30, parade at 11 o'clock & musketry lecture from 11.30 to 12 o'clock when we dine, & then we have the afternoon & evening to ourselves unless we are on guard duty or else orderly duty. I was orderly yesterday; I had to set the tables, get the food from the cookhouse, & then, after we had fed, I had to wash up the tins, scrub the table & brush up any dirt which was near our mess table.

I expect to post this from Alexandria which we will reach on Friday, so our voyage is nearly at an end. It will be a real treat to be able to walk about a Town once more; of course I told you that our destination was Khartum. Yesterday, much to our surprise, a fleet of 20 vessels passed us & we discovered that they were Indian troops on their way to France. Remember me to Pat, Lena & Tom & everybody else. I haven't any more to say now but will write you again when we are fairly settled at Khartum.

Thursday

I've just had a fine hot salt-water bath followed by a cold one. We shall have the boat to ourselves tomorrow as 3 Companies are getting off at Alexandria. Have been very busy this morning washing the white paint on the cabins & am now waiting for a scrumptious tea of bread & salt butter.

Alexandria Merchant
Seaman's Home

Friday 25 Sept 1914

We have now left Alexandria & are on our way to Port Said. I have no doubt that you will look with surprise at the heading of this paper, but these are the kind of hotels which a common Tommy is privileged to enter. I was on guard outside this place, my duty being to stop the natives from selling fruit & mineral waters to any of the troops who were ashore & I can tell you I had my work cut out as it's no earthly use talking to them, you have to bring your toe into action and they run away like gibbering monkeys.

Of course we saw the worst part of Alexandria, as we did not go past[†] the docks, & as you know, the docks of any port are the worst part, but the dock labourers here were just like monkeys, dressed up in all kinds of queer garb, & the whole time they were working they made a most horrible babble; it sounded to us as though they were all quarrelling with eachother. The funniest thing was to see the native policemen ordering these fellows about. Each policeman had a whip or stick and they didn't bother talking to them, but simply brought the whip or stick down on them, either across the body or face, whichever was the nearest.

We left here early Friday morning & nothing very exciting happened until Saturday night when we arrived at Port Said about 10 o'clock & stayed until 4 o'clock Sunday morning. We did not see much of the port, being dark, but I should think that round the dock the place would be more picturesque than Alexandria. Whilst we were in Port we all went to the side of the ship & talked to the people on the dockside, although we could not see them. There was one question which struck me as being rather funny: a woman's voice called out in good English ''Is there anybody on board from Stockport?'' So, of course we answered back in

---

[†]"past" meaning "beyond".

chorus "Yes!". I am sorry we did not stay here until daylight as I should like to have seen it by daylight.

I didn't go to bed at all this night as I was very interested watching the different boats come to ours, some with Government Officials & others selling cigarettes & Turkish delight to the troops. After leaving Port Said we entered the Suez Canal, and of course we have land on either side of us, but it is most uninteresting as for miles there is nothing but sand, which becomes very monotonous. Now & then we passed a party of three or four natives travelling across this sand desert on camels. The canal is so narrow in places that two boats cannot pass eachother.

Last night (Sunday) we arrived at Port Suez which is at the other end of the canal, so we didn't do badly to go through it in a day. We stopped here awaiting orders which we received early Monday morning, and steamed away at full speed & we are now in the Gulf of Suez.

There is only one thing which worries me now, & that is how to get rid of these beastly flies which simply swarm round us, & I'm sorry to say that they have taken a particular liking to me ... & even now whilst I am writing they are teasing me to death. The heat here is 115 degrees in the shade, & I am writing this on the floor of the deck with nothing on but a bathing costume which is my daily garb. Every day, in a certain corner of the boat we have a strong hose-pipe, & about three times a day we all go there & play it on eachother. It's delightfully cooling (of course it's salt water).

I forgot to mention that at Port Suez a very exciting incident occurred : in a boat which came alongside there was actually a white woman, the first we had seen since leaving Littleborough (she was the wife of a Government Official) & of course we all flocked to the side of the boat to catch a glimpse of such a rare thing.

This morning the cookhouse went mad – they actually gave us one herring each for breakfast, as ever since leaving Southampton we have had porridge alternate mornings & the other mornings bread & salt butter.

Tuesday Sept 29

Whilst I am writing this I am on guard at the back of the ship with nothing on but my Lacrosse trousers & it's hard work keeping cool. This morning at 2 o'clock Eddie & myself got out of bed & were strolling about the deck with bathing costumes on.

We are now in the Red Sea & have once more lost the sight of land. We have taken the gunboat Mosquito as our escort. We have left all the other 14 boats at different ports and are now on our own. I'm thankful to say that this is our last day on the water as we reach Port Sudan where we disembark and have about 36 hours train ride to Khartum.

I hope you are all keeping well & not worrying about the Chocolate Soldier, as up to now that's what it's been. Of course, as soon as we get to Khartum they will start putting us through it. I should like to know if Father has got my contract money refunded yet & if Turtle House[†] is still the same go-ahead Firm as when I left it.

It is now Wednesday morning 3.30 a.m., a most unearthly hour to be writing letters isn't it, but it means either finishing now or not at all, as we are due at Port Sudan somewhere near 5 o'clock, & we are the first Company to leave the ship, so there is a lot to be done.

You wouldn't know me if you saw me now as I look like a scared convict with my hat off. On account of cleanliness and coolness I've had my hair clipped so short you can see my scalp, & I'm jolly certain you would not know me with my sun helmet on, but I'll send you a photograph as soon as possible.

I haven't time to write more now as I've got to pack & prepare for the 24 hrs train ride which is before us. Has Mr B- sent the pipe yet? If so, don't send it here, but describe it to me in detail so that I can thank him from here. Remember me to them all. Love to Father, Patty & yourself, & remember the old motto that the worm said to the hen.

Postcard

At the present moment I am on guard in the town of Alexandria, but I have just managed to slip in the Post Office for a few seconds to send this postcard. I've never been so hot in my life, there will be nothing left of me in a week.

[†]Turtle House - C.S. Morten's Office in Piccadilly, Manchester.
He was a merchant of collars, mainly the stiff variety.

THE SUDAN

Saturday October 3rd 1914
Khartum

Dear Mother & Father,

We are now settled in the barracks in Khartum & it's a fine place. We spent the day in Port Sudan & it's a most dead alive sort of place, I'm jolly glad we're not stationed there; there is one of our Companies there. I expect that you will have received the letter I posted there, also the enclosure for Thomas[†].

The British Barracks, Khartoum

We left Port Sudan at 9 o'clock on Thursday morning & arrived here yesterday at 2 o'clock so you can tell it's a good way from the coast (about 800 miles). The trains here are like the continental ones, the doors are at the end of each coach, & we were lucky enough to get on

[†]Thomas Hardman of Bury, sister Pat's boyfriend.

the end compartment where the door was so we had a through draught of air which is a luxury in these parts. They have no glass in the windows, but simply a shutter which you can let down for the rain or the sandstorms. There were seven in our compartment, & we had three stops on the way for feeding; at each stop we all got out of the train & took our mess tins with us, and each compartment stood together, then one of the orderlies would get hold of the bread, bully beef & Dutch cheese, then each of us filled our mess tins with tea & then got back onto the train. I wish you could have seen us dishing out & eating the beef & cheese with nothing but the cutlery which nature provided us with (fingers).

At night we all arranged ourselves, some on the floor, others on the seats, stretched out for sleep, & I never slept better in my life. We never had the door closed the whole of the way, not even at night. It's an event that everybody can't say they have done : travelled 800 miles in a train & never had the door closed. We had to pull down the shutters of the windows about three times on account of the sandstorms, the sand blew in & got in your eyes & up your nose, & made you sneeze as though you had had a good dose of electric snuff.

It really was a most memorable ride; for the first part of the journey there was nothing but sand & range after range of hills, absolutely bare with not a particle of vegetation on them. At first they looked really magnificent, as far as you could see, hills rising one above the other in one long range, but it got rather boring. The only thing I can liken them to in England is the scenery round the fireworks at Belle Vue[†] on a very large scale. The second half was rather more varied as here & there you would see a small plantation.

It's really marvellous how the natives live: wherever you saw a native village you would see a flock of goats & a few donkeys & camels. Of course they live to a great extent on goat flesh. The native villages are very picturesque, all built out of mud.

The funniest part of the journey was on the Friday morning as we had instructions to shave & polish the buttons on our tunics so that we should make a good impression when we arrived at Khartum. We had no mirrors & no washing basins, but had to use our mess tins & shave eachother which was rather a precarious business in a small compartment with chaps leaning over you to borrow the brush or the metal polish from someone who had polished his buttons. I can tell you I felt very relieved that I had my safety razor with me.

We were met at the station by the Sirdar[‡], the commander of all the troops in Egypt, & by Jove he had some medals & ribbons! As we passed we all saluted him. We marched from the station to the barracks in the broiling midday sun, & not one of the company dropped out, which is a thing worth mentioning as we are told that when the Suffolks marched from here to the station (the Regulars which we have relieved) three of them dropped out & one died in the train, & they had their thin drill regimentals on, whereas we had our thick khaki uniforms on & full packs, so that's one for the 7th Manchesters.

[†]Belle Vue - an amusement park in Manchester.
[‡]General Sir F.R. Wingate, Bart., G.C.B.,G.C.V.O.,G.B.E.,K.C.M.G., D.S.O.

The Sirdar and Escort

The heat here is terrific; although I'm sitting on my bed writing this I'm perspiring so much that I can wring my shirt, & this is the approach of winter. It's a very lazy life: we rise at about 5.30 a.m. & have a Swedish drill parade, then have breakfast & about 10 o'clock we are dismissed for the day as it's too hot to work after, so we lounge about the barrack room & the grounds.

The grounds are a jolly sight larger than many a village (in fact it is a small village) built on the bungalow style. In the grounds we have our own shop where we can buy everything, a library, sports room, club & writing room. I have not yet discovered the writing room; having been here only a day I haven't quite got my bearings.

I'm pleased to say that we are all together in one room excepting Bill Higgins & he has gone to Cyprus. We also have two blacks to do the washing & keep the room clean, for which each of us pays one piastre (which is equal to one penny & a farthing in English money). The names of our servants are Friday & Babican & they are most charming with their flattened nose & legs like matchstalks. It's a real treat to sit down & know that you haven't to wash

*They did look funny on the
donkeys.*

your own mess tins afterwards. We have several regimental pets
comprising of dogs & monkeys.

The grounds are very pretty as all the different buildings are built
of light stone with various tropical creepers clinging round them.
All the Officers have a mule each for riding on, & some of them
look very peculiar spectacles, for instance Jack Thorpe† with his
long legs which nearly reach the ground. When we feel like a ride
we have donkeys with a most terrible neigh. I've never heard
donkeys neigh like them in all my life. It's like a thunderstorm
when they all begin at once.

The one thing I don't like is the dearness of everything, even the
fruit is abnormally dear. A thing for which you would pay 6d in
England costs you here 1/3. We had dinner on the veranda today
& a huge vulture came & perched about 4 yards from me.

We are all in excellent health except Harold Granger & I'm sorry
to say that I haven't seen him since we arrived here. He was in
hospital the whole of the voyage & he was taken in a kind of
stupor in the train, so they removed him to the Red Cross quarters
& he is now in hospital.

Eddie & Marshall‡ wish to be remembered to you. I am now
having my tea consisting of tea without milk & dry bread. The
barracks here are recognised as the finest in Egypt, of course
Kitchener's doing, & we have some fine shower baths which I
frequently use, & it's most refreshing.

There is one thing which I would like you to do – that is you
might send me one or two hundred cigarettes, Gold Flake will be
quite good enough, as the Virginia cigarettes here are dear &
rotten & I don't like the Egyptian cigarettes.

Remember me to the Brooks & other friends & give my love to
Patty, Tom & Lena. My best love to you & Father. I am now
expecting my man Friday to bring me my washing.

---

†Jack Thorpe, son of the Rector of St. George's Church, Stockport.
‡Eddie Granger and Marshall Bateman.

Saturday October 10th 1914

Dear Pat,

Thanks for the letter which I have just received, it takes an awful long time for letters. Every time a mail arrives there is great excitement because over here we get no news except what comes by letter. How is the War progressing, you might let me know? How did the wedding go off? I bet you felt proud of the groomsman. Tell Mrs N- not to let her tongue wag too much or it might drop off its hinges.

We are all together in one barrack room with a corporal who is one of the funniest chaps you can come across, a real sport. I am sorry Bill Higgins is not with us, but he & Harold Breton have gone to Cyprus. I'm sorry we didn't all go there as it's not so hot and things are as cheap again as they are here. Frank Heyes is with the Cyprus Company.

You talk about the poor children scrapping for food, well it can't be worse than the way we fight for our food, if you can call it such; if you are five minutes late it's all gone. I am now recovering from dinner which consisted of leathery meat & rice pudding made of water. For breakfast we each had a small tin (the size of a threepenny bit) of lobster paste, awful stuff, but it meant eating that or nothing. I never thought that I would go begging for bread, but yesterday, when tea arrived, I discovered that I had eaten my half loaf which is served out at breakfast time for the whole day, & I couldn't buy any, so I had to go round & beg a small piece from each chap, & this kind of thing happens every day.

There are sixty of the Regulars left here to man the guns at the Fort, & they think that the way we are being fed is abominable considering that we are volunteers. They are being fed a jolly sight better. They belong to the Royal Garrison Artillery & one or two of them are ripping sports. Remember me to Tom & the family. Love to Father & Mother.

Yours sincerely
Jack

PS. Don't send the pipe

Tuesday October 13 1914

It would be very acceptable to receive some news from home as, up to writing, I've only received one small letter from Mother & Patty, & out here we get very little news.

Today Lieutenant Whitley (the Lacrosse player) gave us a Stockport Advertiser & I read with great regret the death of Mr Thomas Kay.

I'm not writing very much this time as the object of this letter is an appeal which I have no doubt you will respond to with your usual generosity to the needy ones. The Territorial Army is carried on in a most unsympathetic fashion. They owe us about 30/- back pay, & instead of having a weekly system of paying, they pay us when the fit takes them. It is now Tuesday & I've only got $2^{1}/_{2}$ piastres ($6^{1}/_{2}$d) to last me until Saturday. I hope you won't think me extravagant, because I'm not spending a farthing more than is necessary. All our pay, when we get it, goes on eatables; yesterday a deputation from the men was sent to the Officers to see what could be done in the feeding line. It's above a joke when you have to beg bread for tea (now we can buy it from the canteen as they see there is a demand). The first day I asked them if they sold bread they informed me that they had never been asked for it before, so the first week we were here it was a case of finding out the ones with small appetites & begging a piece from them. So you will not think me extravagant, I will tell you a few of the things I require, with the cost of them out here. They are as follows:

An enamel cup 1/3

1 pr pumps for Lacrosse 5/-

a padlock for my kit bag 2/- etc.

You will see from these prices that things are pretty dear out here. I've spent my last piastre on a luxury so that it would not be a case of dry bread for tea & breakfast. The luxury is a two pound tin of Lyle's golden syrup, for which Harry & myself paid 1/3 and we spread it on our bread very sparingly as it's got to last a week. We are not quite certain whether the back money the Army owes us will be paid to us here or will be saved until after the War then given to us in the form of a grant when we arrive home. In the meantime the whole lot of us are stony, so under the circumstances a *quid* or *two,* or should I say a pound or two, will be very acceptable.

Before closing I might as well tell you that I've had a very nice letter from Mr Joel Taylor which was also signed by about twenty of the Institute members including Mr Twyford[†] & Mr Holt.

I believe they will change English postal orders at the Khartum Post Office. Awaiting anxiously your early reply.

Khartum
Monday Oct 19 1914

Dear Pattie,

Thanks for your letter which I received yesterday by the last mail. I wrote Aunt Alice &

[†]Mr Twyford was involved with the lads at the Mount Tabor Chapel in Stockport.
C.S. Morten was an official of the church and for 45 years its treasurer.

from what Mother said about the letters going round I expect you will have read it, so there is not really very much to tell you as the life here is the same day after day.

Last night (Friday) our Battalion band was engaged to play in the gardens of the Royal Hotel. The hotel is a palatial place with beautiful gardens & seven of us went to listen to it, & for the moment I thought I was in the Midland† drinking lovely iced drinks. We sat there all night & it was a real treat, as our band is recognised as the finest in Manchester, and they gave us all a selection from the musical comedies.

In Father's last letter he asked me if Barratt & Breton were here, well Barratt is, but Breton has gone to Cyprus with Bill Higgins & Lieutenant Hayes.

We had our first Lacrosse meeting last week, Major Staveacre presiding, and as he said, in time to come it will be quite historical as we are the first team which has ever played Lacrosse in the Sudan. The Sirdar we made patron, our Colonel President and Lieutenant Whitley Captain, Captain Smedley vice-Captain, Barratt secretary & Bateman, Eaton, Brown,

The Lacrosse Team

†The Midland Hotel in Manchester

Smith & myself on the committee, so it will be rather an honour to say that you were on the committee of the first Lacrosse team in the Sudan, won't it ? (bow-wow).

I'm having some very funny experiences; for instance for three days last week I hadn't a single farthing in my pocket, couldn't even buy a packet of cigarettes, & couldn't borrow a cent from any of the boys because they were all in the same boat. I've often been stony at home, but there I could always borrow from a friend or *relation*. On Friday we were paid amidst great excitement, so on Saturday we were able to have our usual steed (donkeys) to Khartum and there had a feed to commemorate it. I had the first decent feed I've had since leaving England. It consisted of cutlets, peas & chips with semolina pudding & iced water. There was only one drawback, and that was the shortness of it, but I ate very slowly and made it last as long as possible. The way the waiter looked at us I think he thought that we had bought the table, so we thought it was time to be going home.

On arriving at our mess in the Barracks there was great excitement in the shape of a mouse-hunt, so we armed ourselves with broomsticks and joined in, and as fast as we killed one another came along. At last we finished them all off then made our beds & retired for the night.

It's rather strange you haven't seen Beatty[†]. Hadn't you better call & have afternoon tea with them & arrange about Port Erin for next year?

Tell Father that I made a mistake about the contract when I said there would be some money to come back. I don't know what I was thinking about as the arrangement was that I pay every month, so naturally the months that the contract had still to run are not yet paid, so it's quite all right. When I wrote about the contract it was on board that awful boat, so it's quite excusable my making a slight error.

I'm going to have my photograph taken and will send one or two as soon as possible. They are not half putting us through it. Now we are all under regular instructions and I should say that during the week we have had them, we have improved in discipline and smartened ten times to what we would do in a month under the Territorial's Sergeant.

Every morning at half past 9 we have our mess rooms inspected by the Captain, Adjutant and one or two other knuts, and three times we have been complimented on our mess room being the most tidy in the Company.

I suppose Aunt Alice told you about the soldier's funeral[‡] which we attended. Well yesterday we had an auction sale of his personal belongings & kit, the proceeds to be sent home to his widow, & it realised quite a good sum.

[†]Beatrice, his girlfriend.
[‡]Ernest Kenyon; he died of dysentery.

Lieutenant Thorpe has been in hospital now for a week, also the Colonel, but I am pleased to say that we are all right. Harold Granger has now come out.

Before closing I would like to remind you that a newspaper out here is quite a luxury, so you might send me one every so often, also, next time you write, give me a little War news. Remember me to Harrisons, Fletchers, Brooks etc and by the way, tell Katy that her friend Mr William Moss is in our mess, & we kid the life out of the poor chap. Give my best love to B-, Father, Mother & Lena. Hoping that you are all well and keeping your pecker up. Harry sends his kind regards and wishes you to convey to Doris his *best love.*

Monday Oct 26th
Khartum

Dear Father,

I hope this letter will find you all very well, as it leaves me in that condition. You don't say much about business in your letters. Have you not had any jackinette† orders yet? We are pipping the Germans nicely, are we not?

My letters from now will be somewhat shorter than previously, as there is not so much variety to write about as there was on the boat when we were calling at a fresh place every week, but here one day is like another; the only way I manage to count the days is by pay-day which is on a Friday, & by Tuesday we are all looking forward to Friday coming round.

I mentioned in a previous letter that some money would be very acceptable; I hope that by the time you receive this you will have sent the same on to me, as it is a very valuable asset in a place like this where things cost you double, and in some cases treble the amount they would be in England. At the present moment I would give anything for a common "Wild Woodbine" cigarette, as it's quite out of the question buying decent Virginia cigarettes here.

I had a newspaper & letter from Mrs Harrison by the last mail. No doubt you will be pleased to hear that Lieutenant Thorpe is now out of hospital.

Yesterday, being Sunday, we had a church parade at 6.15 in the morning, of course in the open air, & for one of the hymns we had the Anniversary hymn "All hail the power of Jesus' Name". It seemed quite strange singing it under the altered conditions.

At night Baty‡, Harry & myself rode on donkeys to the Cathedral where we had a very nice English service, afterwards going to the Lord Byron Cafe where we had coffee & cakes, then we rode back to the Barracks.

---

†Jackinette - a type of fabric.

‡Baty - Marshall Bateman. He is usually referred to by this nickname.

This afternoon I had a nice walk along the side of the Blue Nile. Along the banks there are some very nice gardens, but the most unique part is the manner in which they are watered. There is a trench dug all round the garden, & on the bank of the river there are two bullocks with a negro sat behind them, & all day long these bullocks walk round & round in a circle working a cog which works another, & it lowers buckets into the river; when they are full they come up in their circular route & the water is emptied into the trenches where it runs round the garden. I can't describe it very well, but the same methods were used in the days of Adam & Eve.

Raising water 'Biblical' style

Last night we had a lecture by Lieutenant Thorpe on General Gordon, followed by a concert in which the band & the men who could sing or recite took part. I would have given a turn but I had no music; a song like "Drake goes West" or "Lighterman Tom" would have gone down well.

I've just finished some of Miss Wood's Lemon Roll & chocolate which Bert Smith had sent to him, & I can tell you I didn't half relish it. I've had my photograph taken, but it isn't a good one so I'm having it retaken. I expect you will be preparing for Xmas now; it will be rather a funny Xmas out here especially if we have our usual Stew for Xmas Dinner.

I must close now as I've rather a lot to do, what with darning socks & cleaning my rifle etc. We had some good sport this morning in the shape of bayonet practice. We had the bayonets with the spring tops, like the ones they have on the stage, so that when you bayonet your opponent, instead of sticking him, the spring simply goes in, but all the same it's jolly good practice. Don't forget the cash. Give my love to Mother, Patty, Tom & Lena. Remember me to everyone else. The boys wish to be remembered to you.

Saturday October 31st 1914
Khartum

Dear Mother,

I have just received your letter of the 14th for which I thank you. I am pleased to hear that you are all very well. I would like to see Alf Cauldwell & Stanley Sutton drilling. It won't be half bad going to Southport for the winter, will it? I am glad you are sending me some newspapers.

It's very strange that nothing has been heard of the 6th. Their boat travelled with us as far as Alexandria, but after leaving that port I can't tell you where they went. In your letter you ask me who I slept near, well, Jack Hulme, Frank Lomas, Eddie, Marshall, Bert Smith, Wilfred Sykes, Jack Richardson, Walter Manning, the two Hollands & myself are altogether forming a kind of square.

In reply to your question "Would I like a Xmas Cake?" well, I should jolly well think I should, the bigger the better, as it's so rare we taste anything so delicious as one of your own special lines in Xmas Cakes. Also one or two packets of Velma†. You had better send the Xmas parcel as soon as you receive this, as it takes such a time for parcels to come & I should be terribly disappointed if it wasn't here for Xmas day.

Yesterday was the Xmas Day here for the natives & rather an exciting episode happened in connection with it. I don't know whether I told you but about 20 yards from the Barracks is the Fort with its huge guns ready to blow Khartum up in case of any trouble with the natives. Our instructions are that on hearing three blanks fired from a cannon followed by three rockets, we have to immediately put on our equipment, get our guns & as much as we can of our kit & fall in ready to march to the Fort, as this is the sign of a native uprising. The night before last we were talking so peaceably in the Barracks when all of a sudden we heard this

†Velma - Swiss dark chocolate.

alarm. Well, you've no idea how I felt as I rushed for my equipment, all excitement, but we soon discovered that it was a false alarm, as instead of firing only three, the guns fired about twenty, & we then learned that they were only saluting the arrival of Xmas Day.

I have received Pat's letter of the 5th & I must say it's very *interesting* to read that she has got a black velour hat. From what she says you seem to have some very exciting "At Homes" with the various mothers.

Pat also informs me that Tom wishes to buy some tobacco, well some Chairman tobacco will go down jolly well, & you might tell him from me that I always said he was a sport, & this very kind action on his part absolutely proves my saying.

I'm glad to hear that Douglas Stephenson is improving. I have a suggestion here from Eddie. He intended putting it in his letter to his people but forgot, so he asked me if you would tell Mrs G-. He proposes that anything all you mothers are sending for Xmas be sent to the bon-bon works† in small parcels & there they will be put into a case & sent along, thereby costing less money for carriage & being a jolly sight stronger way of packaging; of course it's simply a proposal on Eddie's part.

I must close now as being Saturday I'm going to Khartum tonight. Tell Aunt Alice I received her P.C. with thanks. Give my love to Pat, Father & Lena & Tom. Kind regards to everybody else, & best love to yourself.

Jack

PS. I'm sending this without a stamp as they are sold out at the canteen & there is a rumour that we are allowed to send them without. Let me know if you pay on it.

PS. I hope that you have attended to the urgent appeal which I made in the previous letter regarding money.

Khartum
Wednesday Nov 4th 1914

I am only writing a short letter to you this time, on account of both shortage of time & news. When you write you might let me know the date of the last letter you have received before posting mine so that I shall know the exact time it takes for letters to come.

I'm enclosing a photo which is not a very good one as the sun was in my eyes. I've had another one taken in full uniform, which, when I receive them I will send along to you & several other friends in Stockport. I have sent one of the enclosed to Mrs Brooks & Aunt Alice but I don't think I shall send any more away because I don't think they are good.

†John Horn & Co. Stockport.

In my last letter I omitted to state that some parkin† would be very acceptable in my Xmas parcel.

In your letter of the 9th ulto you state that either Eddie or Marshall have some lighter clothing for me, well I think you are mistaken, as both of them know nothing about it; I might add that the pants & vests I brought with me are no good, being too thick. I wear no underclothing except the two shirts which I brought with me, one for night & the other for day, but they will be soon worn out, as with perspiring so much I have them washed pretty frequently & the niggers don't half scrub them. It's worse than the Shaw Heath Laundry for washing your things to nothing. Some long light undervests would be very acceptable to wear in place of a shirt, or else one or two light shirts. I simply wear my body belt at night, as over here we are not advised to wear them in the daytime.

I'm sorry to hear about Tom & hope that by the time you receive this he will be restored to his full jocular spirits.

In Father's letter of the 11th ulto he informs me that James has left him, but he doesn't say why. You might tell Father to write a few more details when he writes, as a *good correspondent never misses detail.*

I have enclosed a photograph for my old pal Mrs Hardman which I have no doubt Tom will deliver. Trusting you are all jolly well.

I'm sending this without a stamp, as I understand that as we are on foreign service we are allowed to do so. Let me know if you have to pay. It's a terrible job trying to buy a stamp here; they are always sold out, so I'm risking it without.

Khartum
November 12 1914

This is in reply to yours of 20th ulto. I am pleased to hear that you are all in good health & that you have received my first letter from here.

I pity the poor beggars who have to drill with Lieutenant Astle. I hope that Tom is all right now.

Last week one night, instead of the afternoon parade we had night operations. It was a pitch dark night & the whole Company was marched out in full marching order (which is, bayonet, rifle & pouches with 20 rounds of ammunition) across the desert. When we were right in the desert we split up, one half of the Company marched out, & after a lapse of ten minutes we had to track them & creep on our stomachs without them seeing us. It was most funny, especially as you will no doubt know that in night operations all the orders are given in a

†Parkin - a sticky dark gingerbread made with oatmeal.

whisper & they are passed down the ranks by the men. Well just my luck, the man next to me happened to be deaf, so every order that was given I had to give him a jolly good dig in the ribs.

On Tuesday night we had a concert with a very varied programme. The band played a selection for the overture, then followed Captain Smedley with a song (he has a glorious voice). This was followed by a supposed-to-be-tragic recitation by a corporal entitled "A most villainous Plot". He stepped up onto the platform with the swank of a Lord & announced the title of his recitation. This is the way he pronounced it after bowing & smiling at everybody – "A most villaynyous Plot". I began to feel that my education had been neglected as every big word he came across had a fresh pronunciation.

Today is Thursday & I'm on guard for 24 hours at the hospital gate, 2 hrs on & 4 off, but I cannot go to the mess during my 4 hrs off, as during this time I have to be in the guardroom & try to catch what sleep I can which is very little, as we are not allowed to pull our equipment off & there is nothing to lie on but hard boards, & every time you are dozing off you hear the sentry who is on guard yell out "Guard turn out!" & you have to spring up like grease lightning, get your rifle & line up outside with the other guards who are taking their four hours off, & present arms to the Colonel or some other big knut†. We always have to do this for the Colonel, Sirdar, Orderly Officer & armed parties, so you can tell if one of these knuts takes it into his head to walk past the guard room two or three times, we are kept pretty busy.

The worst part of this job is the night. I am on from 11 o'clock p.m. until 1 o'clock a.m. so I am looking forward to a good time, all on my own, parading up & down the thick shrubbery which surrounds the hospital, the stillness of the night broken only by the barking & yelping of the desert dogs which invade the Barrack grounds at night in the hopes of finding a spare meal.

I've just had a funny experience: I was seated on the throne‡ (the House of Parliament, you know) & I felt something jump onto my shoulder & cling round my neck. I looked up & much to my horror & amazement I saw there a monkey which had jumped over the wall. At first it rather startled me, especially as I saw by the way it settled down that it meant to stay there, but by the time it went we had got quite friendly. It was about the neatest & prettiest little monkey I have seen, it being no bigger than a kitten.

I'm now off for my two hours duty so will finish this in two hours time. I'm now off duty again so will continue this short narrative. The Barracks at present are full of convicts in the daytime. There are over a thousand here making alterations, & each one has chains on his legs, & they don't half work. They are the most foul bloodthirsty looking fellows I ever saw.

---

†Knuts - Big-wigs.
‡The toilet.

You might tell Lena that I think the photo is splendid & if I didn't happen to know the original I should have taken it for a maid of sweet sixteen.

The Xmas Cake, pudding & tin you mention will be jolly acceptable. Thank Father for the cigarettes which you say he has sent, although they are not yet to hand. Now for one hrs sleep.

Khartum
Nov 24th 1914

This is in reply to your welcome letter of the 5th ulto. Today I received the registered letter with the necessary enclosed, so I am as happy as a young sparrow, in fact Eddie, Marshall, Harold & myself & several others in the mess have received tin† by today's post, so for the present there is no holding us back.

†Tin - tiffin - goodies.

No doubt you will have noticed that I am now writing in a civilised way, namely ink instead of pencil, pen & ink being the first purchase with my new state of finance. I am pleased to inform you that our conditions are greatly improved now we are settled down, especially in the food line. Here is a rough outline of the daily menu:

Breakfast

One morning liver & onions, the next porridge, the next tinned salmon or herrings. We have these on alternate mornings (not all on one, we are not at Belle Vue, Port Erin).

Dinner

Soup & stewed steak with peas or other vegetables which I cannot name, as when it is served up it resembles grass; I imagine it's a vegetable only grown in Khartum. Then the next day, by way of a change, we have the same kind of meat served up in the form of a steak pie, but we kid ourselves that it's different until our teeth get into it, and occasionally we have macaroni pudding.

Tea

Bread & stewed tea only, so I always have a stock of jam or syrup in, & on Sunday, by way of a special treat, two of us whack at a small tin of sardines or stewed fruit, but I would sacrifice jam or stewed fruit any teatime for a good plate full of nicely cut home made bread & butter. Butter can be bought here, but from reports of chaps who have tried it, I am quite satisfied to go without it.

Then, with regards to pay, we are now getting our thirty-seven piastres regularly on a Friday, & every month we get Khedives pay so I have just managed to exist frugally. On reading this you might think that I've been extravagant, but when you take into consideration that in most cases, especially in eatables, that what you buy at home for a penny, out here costs you a piastre, you will come to the conclusion that thirty-seven piastres is a great deal more on paper than in reality. Fresh eggs can be bought quite reasonably off the natives ($^1/_2$ piastre each or $1^1/_4$d) and for the last fortnight I've had about six a day, as I beat them up & have them raw in my tea, which makes a jolly good substitute for milk. I am investing five piastres in a small spirit stove, so most likely when you receive this I shall be having fried, poached, boiled & all kinds of egg dishes.

With regard to the above menu, usually the dinner is the worst on account of the meat being so tough, but in that case I make up for it in jam; I pity some of the poor chaps with rotten teeth. More than one has broken them when struggling with a piece of steak. But today they have started a new system: we had pie, & when opened we discovered that the meat was minced, & it was a decided improvement.

Now to change the topic: we have now been busy on the rifle range for the last week or so, every morning from 5.30 until 8.30. I've passed my standard test for shooting at 500 yards; I got one bullseye, three inners & one outer, not so bad seeing that I have not done much shooting, is it?

Here is a diagram of the target & it looks jolly small at five hundred yards:

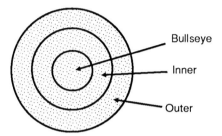

Now the weather is cooler we are fairly going through it. I say cooler, but this only applies in the early morning & the evening. In the morning it just feels as though it were freezing, although the thermometer never registers less than 60° but it seems colder in comparison with the midday heat.

Yesterday morning for three and a half hours before breakfast we were transformed into navvies. The whole of our Company marched onto the desert with rifles, pick-axes & spades. Arriving there we were ordered to stack our rifles then set to work to dig a trench about 20 yards long & 4ft 6ins deep. I can tell you that by the time we had finished we all felt ready for our breakfast.

Tonight we are having a night skirmish on the desert but Baty, Barratt, Norbury & myself are exempt from it as we are on guard at the Sirdar's Palace tomorrow, & for this you have to turn out spick & span, so I look like having a busy time polishing buttons, cleaning boots etc.

Lieutenant Thorpe has now returned & is now the Lieutenant in charge of our platoon.

By the last mail I received letters from Arnold, Janet Barlow & Mrs Joe Smith, and a paper from Mrs Harrison, so when you see these people you might thank them & tell them they were greatly appreciated. Of course I shall write to them all myself, but I have not the time to write them all at once. I also received some Daily Mirrors without any name on, so I presume you sent them from home.

You say that Father has sent me two hundred cigarettes, well I have received two hundred, but on opening same there was a card inside which said on it ''with Mr Mercer's compliments'' so naturally I concluded that he had presented them to me. In your next letter you might say whether Mr Mercer or Father has sent them, then I shall know who to thank. I should very much appreciate a letter from Father saying how the business is & why Sandy left. I have joined the regimental tennis club.

Khartum
Sunday Dec 3rd 1914

Dear Patty,

Thanks for your letter of the 9th. I received letters from Mrs Smith & little Josie, Edith & Wilson, Katie, Arnold Williams, Janet Barlow & Dick, also 100 cigarettes from Dick & Marion – jolly sporty of them, wasn't it? Dick also said if there was anything else I required I must let him know & he would send it. When you come across any of the above, thank them for me, because I can't write to all of them at once.

I also received the Sunday Chronicle, The War Illustrated, & the four Manchester Guardians which have kept me busy for days thoroughly digesting them. I was greatly surprised at hearing of Nora Stephenson's engagement, whoever he is, he goes in for quantity, & as far as quantity goes, this time he's struck oil (poor chap). The photo of Marshall is jolly good; would you believe it, I've had my photo taken four times & each one has been a failure; I've had some terrific rows about it: two of the photographers brought me the dozen when they brought the proofs, as they said "in order to save time" – well, our opinions differ about them. They thought they were splendid (naturally), but I though otherwise & wouldn't have them, so they had the dozen left on their hands. I'm having it taken again on Saturday & hope to have a decent result; if not I shall give it up as a bad job, having my dial taken in the Sudan. I'm sorry to say they won't be in time for Xmas, as the Xmas mail leaves on Saturday.

Give Cyril & Fanny my heartiest congratulations, also Uncle Tom, & tell him not to fancy himself now that he has got another nephew on his list, as it will cost him more at Birthdays & Xmas. You might also tell Cyril that young Cyril can have my services as a Golf Coacher. I hope Doris Smith's operation has been successful. Father's notes came in jolly handy & I've made good use of it. I banked £2 of it in the Regimental Bank to be withdrawn as required & I've bought 1 pair of socks 1/-, one regular army shirt 4/6 & a knutty pair of pyjamas 6/-. The pyjamas are all wool, are new, & they cost the chap I bought them off 10/-. I bought them off one of my mess pals; the reason he sold them was because he was hard up & the money which he had been advised of as being on the way, had not arrived, so I struck a bargain.

I was very sorry to read about Fred Johnson's death. I'm longing to have a photo of the new dog. I bet it's some rag-time mongrel. Tell Father to give my kind regards to Mr Mercer & Mr Plant.

I had a very interesting day on Sunday: about twenty of us went to Omdurman (of course you will have heard of the Battle of Omdurman). We caught the train at the gate of the Barracks at 9.45, had about $\frac{1}{2}$ hrs ride, then embarked on a ferry steamer & went for $\frac{1}{2}$hrs sail down the Nile, then got the train for Omdurman. The village is a most interesting place & is one of the few places where you can buy real curios. It was a day out: the whole time, from the moment we left the train to getting on again we were absolutely surrounded by natives selling their different wares, & for each article we bought, we argued with them for at least $\frac{1}{4}$hr. The natives are the biggest robbers unhung, & when they ask you a certain price for a thing, if you offer them half, you eventually get it at your own price, especially if you let them see the money. I priced some really exquisite handmade Egyptian bracelets, & when I have saved enough money I shall make another visit there & bring one or two back with me. We arrived back about five o'clock feeling absolutely famished as we could not buy even a piece of bread in Omdurman, but we made up for it on our return.

I'm absolutely in the pink, in fact I've only had one rotten week since I came here & that was the second week. I had diarrhoea for a whole week but am pleased to say that I got rid of it & have not been troubled since. Yesterday a chap out of our mess went into hospital to be operated on for appendicitis. Father might know him, his name is Fitchett & he goes to the United Methodist Chapel, Wellington Road.

The reason I am writing in pencil is because I am writing this in the guardroom being a guard for 24 hrs. I must close now, Wishing Father, Mother, Lena, Tom & yourself a Merry Xmas & a Happy New Year.

I remain
With Best Love
Jack

P.S. I'm not writing to Mother this week, as it's rather a busy week for us, our Company supplying the whole of the guards this week.

Khartum
Dec 10 1914

Dear Father,

The three pounds which you sent I have already acknowledged in my letters to Pat, and have, as you no doubt have read, come in jolly useful. I wish you would say more about the Office when you write. Have you received any jackinette orders yet?

I have bought a pair of shoes with rope soles for playing Lacrosse. With regard to the Tenants, you can tell *Mar* (you know, the third house in Lostock St) that I will bring home some Khartum Rock for her. Give my kind regards to Mr Plant & Mr Mercer and tell them I would rather be back in Manchester going round to the various Warehouses, even if the houses were 20 stories high and I had to call on the top floor of each one, than be out here wasting time.

I have also received letters of the 16th from Mother & Patty & the M/c Guardians 16th, 20th & 21st & several Daily Mirrors & the three songs. I am expecting daily to receive the boxes of Puddings etc which you mention in your letters. Xmas won't be quite so bad out here after all; from various reports I hear that on Xmas Day the different Companies are having turkeys & puddings etc to be followed in the evening by a smoking concert, then most of the fellows in our mess are having puddings etc sent out to them, so we look like having a week or two of good feeding. I don't know how parades will go down after such large meals with not being used to it.

I'm sorry to say that I'm putting on weight & unless something unforeseen happens I'm rather afraid that when I get home it will be rather a difficult problem to solve as to who has the larger corporation†, you or I. It is not with the meat I'm eating, as many a time I go for days without touching meat, but I put it down to the solid bread & extras which I buy. I told you in a previous letter that we could buy eggs, well for the last month or so I've eaten on an average daily, six eggs. They are really enjoyable, made more so I think because I fry them myself on the little stove which I have bought (I'm really an expert fryer & *poacher*). Then apart from eggs I'm rather heavy on jams, I buy a pound jar every two days.

In Patty's letter she says that she has heard from Mrs Smith that I was kicked off a donkey five times in one night, well that is rather an exaggeration, as the night I came off Bert was not with us & somehow or other he has multiplied it by five, but I've got the laugh over him now as the other night he went out on a donkey & was kicked off twice, & not being like myself sensible enough to fall off in a respectable way, has been limping about like a frog with a bad leg since.

I must close now. Wishing you all a Merry Xmas & A Happy New Year.

Khartum
Dec 19 1914

Dear Mother,

I am in receipt of your letter of the 23rd, also the Xmas parcel which was jolly acceptable. I have also received a letter from Patty dated the 23rd in which she tells me you went to see

†corporation - stomach.

"Milkie Bard", how do you like him? I'm rather afraid that you are getting too giddy in your old age; I expect to hear of you going to the Stockport Empire† next. Well, even that is a jolly sight better than staying in the house reading War news.

I'm pleased to hear that Tom is busy, but Patty has my deepest sympathy only seeing him at the weekends. Of course I suppose she takes Mack‡ for a walk now on Wednesday evenings. You can inform the silly person who has been asking you, Mother, if "I have come home yet" that when I do come home, it's just possible that they will get a "thick ear". I haven't very much time, so can't write much now.

I'm sorry to say that on opening puddings I discovered that they were mouldy, but on emptying them out of the dishes, much to my delight, I saw it was simply round the sides & on the top, so I immediately set about scraping them with my knife & had one boiled for yesterday's dinner; it turned out a treat, I never tasted such a delicious pudding in all my life. I thought it best to have them boiled at once before they started to go mouldy again & am having the other one for today's dinner. I think the puddings were packed too soon after being made, so you will know next time you are sending any. The packet of chocolate which was packed with the puddings was also mouldy, but was eaten & relished in spite of it. The cake is in beautiful condition both as regards to looks & flavour, also the block of Cadbury's Milk Chocolate was in good condition; I am enjoying a piece of it now, & the socks are very comfortable wearing.

Tell Lena that she is a good judge of cigarettes (which rather tells a tale) & give her my best thanks. In one of your letters I understood you to say that you were sending parkin. I was just a little disappointed at not finding any parkin enclosed, but when I tasted the cake I felt quite recompensed.

You keep saying in your letters that Mr Brooks would appreciate one from me, well I wrote to them about a month ago, so you might enquire if they have received it. I might here mention that it's very good of you to send me so many papers, but I haven't time to read them all, so in future just send me the M/c Guardian, the War Illustrated, Public Opinion & any other paper which has a special article on the War. The Xmas Punch is jolly good that Father sent me.

I am sending you a photograph along, which I hope you will like. It's the 6th attempt of the photographer.

---

†A Music Hall.
‡The dog

Khartum
Saturday Dec 26th 1914

Xmas Day is now over & I must admit, what with Xmas Eve & Xmas Day taken together I had a real jolly time which far exceeded my expectations, & it absolutely contradicted the old saying that anticipation is better than realisation.

Of course I had not looked forward to it one bit, being the first Xmas I was absent from home & the weather being so much what we would call in England 'mid-summer'. I didn't really realise that Xmas was so near & therefore didn't prepare myself for a good time, but as you will read further on I dropped fairly on my feet (to put it in a slang way).

Last Saturday a concert was held in the Soldier's Institute. I was asked to sing; with my usual modesty I acquiesced & made a great hit, as they would term it, on the Music Halls. It seems very strange that I should have to come so many thousands of miles from home for people to discover the fine points in my voice (bow-wow) but there you are again, it absolutely proves the old proverb that "a Prophet is not honoured in his own Country". I might mention a few artists besides myself whom you know: they were Harold Grainger, Barratt & Captain Smedley & Walter Manning. At last my turn comes: on Private Morten being announced, I step onto the platform & sing "Lighterman Tom". My song being finished I walk back to my seat at the back of the room amidst great bursts of enthusiasm from the audience. Well, I get seated amongst my pals when I hear my name called out by the Parson & Sergeant Major & I have to give an encore, for which I sang "Drake goes West" which was also well received. I might here mention that there were only three encores given & they were Captain Smedley, Mr Doughty (the Chief Constable here) & myself. I don't know whether the dry air has improved my voice, but one or two of the boys who have heard me warble at home admitted that they had never heard me sing so well before, so you will be pleased to see that the name of Morten, which is so much to the fore in *Stockport Society* is not quite pushed to the rear in Khartum.

On Wednesday last the Khartum Racing Club held another meeting, & Baty, Barratt & myself were in the judges' box which is the best view of the course, as we were in the best position for seeing the last & the final spurt of the horses, apart from the view of the grandstand (which is just behind the judges' box) on which are the resident Colonels & Officers with their wives, & I can tell you they are knuts. If Patty had been here she wouldn't have seen a single race, but would have had the time of her life feasting her eyes on the different dresses (some of them conspicuous by the scarcity of material in them). Of course they look very nice, but most of them are no better than dressed-up dolls.

Now we come to Thursday (Xmas Eve) which I had the good luck to spend with the Officers & Sergeants. It is the custom here on Xmas Eve for the Sergeants of the Battalion stationed here to invite the Officers & the English Sergeants on the Egyptian Staff to a smoking concert. For this purpose the gymnasium was decorated for the occasion. Harold Grainger & myself were asked to sing & Walter Manning was the pianist. The three of us had a jolly good time as H- & myself were only called upon for one song each as they had so many artists, & after we had done our turn we sat down amongst the audience & partook of their refreshments. At twelve o'clock the band struck up one or two Xmas hymns, & mince pies were passed round. At two o'clock "God Save the King" was played & those who were capable wished one another a "Merry Xmas". Of course there were one or two who were too full for words, so they simply shook hands. We got back to our mess & found them all asleep, so we went round, woke them up & wished them a "Merry Xmas", then retired for the night.

At the races

Our Xmas dinner far exceeded my expectations. We had turkey, then pork, followed by Xmas pudding & Rum Sauce & of course the usual nuts & oranges & different kinds of stewed fruit. Our cooks absolutely excelled themselves. The afternoon was spent by sleeping off the effects of such a rich meal (not being used to good living) then at night we had a smoking concert. I might mention that ours was the only company which had turkey, & *our* Officers organised it very well.

On Xmas morning Baty & myself had attended the 10 o'clock service at the Cathedral & it was very well packed. The mail came in at a very appropriate time: I received all your newspapers & Xmas numbers, also Xmas cards from various people namely Francis & Edith, Malcolm Lees, Kathleen Smith, Constance, Mr Bateman, Rideals, letters from Jack Dickinson & Marie & Bessie. I received all these on Xmas morning.

The picture of Nelson which Father has sent I have hung over my bed, it looks jolly well. I am sending by this post two cabinet photographs, one is for Mr & Mrs Ellis, I'm not quite sure of their address, so just explain to them why I have not sent it direct. I don't really like them but it seems to be the best that the photographers can do for me, so I've decided to send them & you can judge for yourself whether they are good or not.

In closing I might just mention that I would like some more songs per return. Queen of the Earth, Tommy Lad, I don't suppose, Sincerity & a few others, but don't send Stonecracker John as we have a copy of it here. Hoping you had a jolly good Xmas. With best love to all.

PS. I suppose you will have read in the papers that we have annexed the Sudan. By the time I come home again the map of the World will be practically all *red*. I don't think the Turks will trouble us here as they are too busy on the Continent with the Russians.

POSTCARDS FROM KHARTUM

Sudanese on the White Nile. To Miss Morton From Marshall

Wishing you all a Happy Xmas & the best of good health in the New Year. Jack's getting on A1.

On the Blue Nile, Khartum. To Mr, Mrs & Miss Morten from Herbert.

Had a very jolly Xmas here but it seems very funny having no snow, mud or rain like you are having at home. Wishing you all a very happy New Year. All are well including myself.

A native hut in Gambela. To Mr & Mrs Morten from Jack

I haven't time to write a letter as we've had rather a big day but I will tell you more about it by the next mail in my letter. Tomorrow I'm going to the Palace. Remember me to them all.

Native shops at Khartoum. To Mr & Mrs Morten from Jack

I wish you & Father a Merry Xmas & a Happy New Year & hope you will have a good time on Xmas Day as we expect to. Best Love

Pilgrims from Warfour on their way to Mekka. To Mr Hardman & Miss Morten from
Jack.

Wishing you a Merry Xmas & a Happy New Year

The Return of H.E. The Sirdar to Khartoum. To Mr & Mrs Morten from
Jack

Just a line to inform you that I've applied for a commission in the Army, of course I've not got my papers to sign yet, & the odds are that I never shall, but if this war lasts a long time I don't like being a private for so long. J Staveacre & H Smedley think we stand a good chance. Will write more by the next mail. Let me know if you approve by return.

Bird's-eye View, Khartoum. To Mr & Mrs Morten from Jack.

You will have to be content with only a P.C. this mail. I'm pleased to say that the exam is over. Up to writing I haven't heard officially whether I've passed or not, but I think I'm safe in my opinion that I have. However I shall know definitely by the next mail. I had quite a surprise packet last week. Mr Hallowell sent Eddy, Marshall, Bert, Harold, Sykes & myself a large box of cigarettes each (about 200 in a box). It's jolly decent of him, isn't it? I'm enclosing one or two photographs. I've received the parcel of shoes. The white canvas shoes are just the thing. Kind regards to all. Best love.

Gordon College, Khartoum. To Pat from Jack

I've just received your letter saying that you have got rid of Mac. Well, to put it mildly, I'm most annoyed, as from the various accounts you have given me of him, I quite think he was the very dog for me. You had better look out for another one, same breed. I had one out here, but its life with me was a very short one. I'll tell you more about it by the next mail. I'm in a big hurry as I'm off now to play the 2nd round of the Tennis Tournament. I'm in the pink, hoping you are the same. Let me know if you have to pay.

Khartoum
January 2nd 1915

Dear Mother & Father,

I've just time to write a short letter before the post goes. For the last two weeks all my spare time has been spent in letter writing, I've had so many to reply to. I hope you enjoyed your Xmas & New Year festivities. I had to give the Watch Night Service a miss this time as I was on guard duty at the Palace, but you will be pleased to hear that I got the "Stick". I don't suppose you will understand this expression, so I will explain. There were four of us put on guard. In the morning, before going on duty, we are paraded before the Adjutant who puts us through a very close inspection, seeing that our rifle, equipment, boots etc are clean. The one whom he considers looks the smartest & cleanest he gives the "Stick" which means to say that instead of doing Sentry in turn with the other guards, you simply look after their meals & get them anything they require from the Canteen, as they are not permitted to leave the guardroom during their 24 hrs duty. The advantage of getting it is that you get your usual night's sleep & you are free to roam about the Barracks instead of having to do the monotonous duty of a Sentry every four hours. I was particularly pleased as I had spent the whole of the previous night cleaning my equipment etc, so my efforts were rewarded.

During the last week I received the tin of parkin etc. The parkin, which is now finished, was delicious, & the pot of veal & ham I'm having for tonight's tea. The OXO I find very good for sleeping on & usually have a cup before retiring for the night.

I think I told you I had a monkey, a fine little animal & most intelligent. I called it "Chico" which is the Arabic for little. On Xmas day Chico was having a morning run & it jumped onto a live wire in the garden of the electrical station & was electrocuted. I was very sorry as I should most certainly have brought it home.

On New Year's Day I received a letter from Mr & Mrs Brooks & Father, a New Testament, a box of cigarettes & a very nice pocket wallet from Mr Twyford & the Men's Bible Class. In my birthday parcel you might enclose two cards of "Batchelor's Buttons", you know – those that do not require stitching on. Mr Mercer will know where you get them from, they are 1d a card. You might tell Mr Twyford that I will write to him at the first opportunity. You might also enclose a pair of rubber canvas shoes for Lacrosse & Tennis, size $8\frac{1}{2}$ or 9. Remember me to all the Hardman's, Ellis's, Brooks, Fletchers etc. Love to yourselves, Patty & Lena.

PS. Don't enclose any more matches in the parcels as the authorities don't like it. I had no trouble with mine but one of the fellows had. You can fill up the corners of the parcels with "Woodbines".

January 8th 1915

I've just time to write you a short letter. Since Xmas I've done nothing in my spare time & I'm just about fed up with scribbling letters.

In your letter dated Dec 10th you say that you have sent me some pyjamas, vests & shirts, but I haven't received them yet; you also state that Father has sent me a sovereign for Xmas, well that is not yet to hand & I'm jolly sure it's time they were here if you sent them on the dates mentioned.

I received the periodicals Father sent including Holly Leaves, Chambers etc. The picture of Nelson I have hung over my bed & it gives the Mess quite a homely appearance in contrast to the bare walls. I hope Patty's boil doesn't spread, because if it starts on a circular route tour she might find it hard to sit down.

Now I hear that S. Alexander & Aubrey Crate-egg are at the front I feel sure that the Kaiser's days are numbered.

You say that you are knitting a khaki muffler, well about the only use I could put it to would be to put on after playing Lacrosse, but now that the summer is advancing I don't think I shall require it.

In Pattie's letter she said that the 200 cigs were from Father & not from Mercer, so now my mind is at rest. I thought that Old Mercer was going beyond his limit in being so generous.

You will be surprised to hear that I had a card wishing me a merry Xmas from Queenie Broadhurst, jolly decent of her isn't it? I don't think I shall have the luck to come across Alan Preston as we are the only Battalion here except for 50 R.G.A. men who are at the Fort. It's jolly decent of Mrs Smith to make me a cake & I'm anxiously awaiting the arrival of the same.

I see that I have been mentioned in dispatches, namely Jack Thorpe's letter in the Express†. I've had a long letter from Mrs Brooks and a PC from Tommy Hellawell.

Yesterday we had a jolly good game of Lacrosse. I was on Major Staveacre's side & needless to say we won. There was quite a crowd of natives watching & it was most amusing: every time one of us got a good check they cheered like fury, especially if one of us got a crack on the head.

†Actually the Advertiser, December 18 1914

NEWS FROM KHARTUM

The Stockport Boys in Egypt

Extract from a letter received this week by the Vicar of St. George's, Stockport, from his son, Second Lieut. J. H. Thorpe, who is serving in the 7th Battalion Manchester Regiment, now in Khartum. Many of the members of the regiment hail from Stockport :-

I got back to Khartum on Sunday, 22nd November, after an absence of six weeks from my own company, during which time I was commanded by General Dysentery. Monday was my first day on parade, and I found a very pleasant surprise in seeing my platoon (a command of sixty men) for the first time. It reminded me of a walk up Bramhall Lane on a Sunday after church, for I have all the Stockport boys in the platoon. I need not tell you that in consequence it is the smartest command in the battalion. The girls in Stockport won't know their old friends when they get back, and will think a Guards Regiment is quartered near the "Jolly Sailor." The Grangers are now dashing soldiers with cavalry moustaches; Bateman is a Hercules, and young Kay is as straight as a poker. Two of our boys, Draper and Bowden, are in the Camel Corps, and look, I expect, with some contempt on an infantry platoon. I hear they are doing very well, and will be going on a trek soon.

The platoon did a very fine performance on Monday morning. At daybreak we sallied out into the desert and dug a big trench before breakfast. I don't think many of us used to rise in Stockport at 5 a.m., but we do here, and soon afterwards you could see Herbert Smith, Morten, Jack Richardson, Shaw, and the rest of them with picks and shovels chucking the sand out of a five-foot trench and no breakfast until 9 a.m. They have a good many rough edges to put up with after comforts at home, but they stick it like men. Their people at home should know that ours are the (probably) best barracks in the Empire, and we have a very fine hospital in case anyone should go sick. Our lads do not manufacture complaints like old soldiers, so when there is one I know it is genuine. The weather is very nice now, and we will all keep fit. If the Turks come here they will get a bit of Davenport Dash; and if we go to Germany, as we all hope, it will be a good bit of St. George's parish fighting for St. George and old England. You will have your troubles at home in the New Year, few I hope, but let no one be anxious about the boy in The Sudan. He is all right.

I've been on the range all morning; there was an absolute gale blowing, & with the beastly old sand filling your eyes & nostrils one nearly imagined they were at Blackpool.

I don't know whether I've told you but we see some most realistic "Mirages" here, especially in the morning. Looking from the Barracks towards the shooting range, a distance of about 1200 yards, it looks just as though the range was on the brink of a huge lake which stretched for miles, but when you get there you discover that it is simply a myth as there is no water at all, so I can quite understand now how many a poor thirsty traveller, having lost his way, has lost his life in making for one of these "Mirages"; it's really wonderful & one can't imagine how realistic they are until you see them.

This morning we had a three hours route march before breakfast with full packs on & 20 rounds of ammunition in our pouches. Today, being Saturday, I am having my usual weekly ride into town.

Khartum
January 13 1915

Dear Father,

Your welcome letter of 22 ulto to hand. The parcel containing 3 Wolsey vests, 2 print shirts, 2 pyjamas & the collars I received yesterday. By the way the collars are no use as collars are worn only by *gentlemen* not Tommys, but the other contents I shall find very useful, and I hope that no more will be required whilst I'm here as I'm now set up for 8 months or so. During this period I sincerely hope that the final spoke will be put into the wheels of the Germans.

With regard to the Xmas parcels, I've already acknowledged same in previous letters which you will have received by now. I'm more than pleased to hear that Mother is now more cheerful & contented, & you can tell her from me that there is absolutely nothing to worry about, as I'm in the pink of condition, & the Government having granted us another 3d a day per man for feeding, the daily grub has greatly improved. I usually have a good breakfast consisting of liver & onions. Added to this I mix 3 fried eggs which I buy myself. For dinner I simply have two spoonfuls of macaroni pudding, because with the cooking appliances we have, if the Government allowed us another 2/- per day extra it would not make the meat tender. Tea, we have either jam or tinned stuff such as herrings or sardines. Now comes supper; for this meal I usually have 3 eggs & onions, of course this last meal we have to buy ourselves. The reason we have liver for breakfast five times out of seven is because, fortunately, the natives won't touch it, owing I think to some religious order. You see I'm not doing at all badly now, in fact I'm getting so fat I've left off having eggs in my tea.

I expect you will have received the photo by now. What do you think of Moss's letter in the Advertiser? The white duck trousers he talks about were never white, & to see him in them you'd think he was a racing knut down on his luck. We've kidded the life out of the poor chap about that letter. Of course I give you credit to have more nouse (as you would say) than to publish any of my letters.

I take it that your new Agency is a buying agency. I only wish I were there to sow the seeds which I hope will mature into a jolly good thing. I note you have taken up some shares in the Government loan; according to the papers there appear to be some good shares on the market.

The reason I haven't sent picture postcards is because I thought you would appreciate letters more, but I will vary my correspondence with a PC when I haven't much to write about. The Grangers are in the pink, also Baty. Bert Smith is the only one who is down in the dumps (don't tell his people).

With this post I'm sending you two newspapers. This is a new thing, got up entirely by our Battalion, and is the 1er all British paper published in the Sudan†.

Khedives pay amounts to 15/- per month, but when several deductions have been made such as 1/- laundry, Barrack Room Damages (which consists of broken electric globes, brushes etc) sports & barber, this item is somewhat reduced.

I hear that Mr Tom Plant has received some good orders from the Italian firm, but that the Italian Government would not allow then to leave the country, rather rotten luck, isn't it? By the way, now that Mercer has come into *our* Firm again, have you taken over his Agency? I hope you have.

On Saturday we have a big day, namely:- along with the Sudanese & Egyptian Troops we are going to be reviewed by the Sirdar. On Sunday Lady Wingate has invited our Battalion only to tea at the Palace; the Officers are not invited, only the NCO's & men.

I have now joined the Signalling section of the Battalion. I got wind of the fact that they were wanting a few more men, so spoke to the Sergeant Major about it, & Baty, Walter Manning & myself have joined. Eddie is not with us as he has joined the Mekometer section. It will be most interesting, but I will tell you more about it when I have done more. From now until the end of February I'll have to put in full time, as there is an examination in February which I have to pass. The one great advantage we have is that we are now exempt from guards, so if I pass the Exam (which I intend to) I shall have finished with the monotonous duty of a Sentry.

I don't know whether you hear any wild ridiculous reports in Stockport, but yesterday Lieutenant Whitley showed me a cutting from a Berlin Paper which had been sent to him,

†The Seventh Manchester Sentry. There seem to have been six issues. It was published here and in Sinai in 1916.

which said that all the Britishers in Khartoum had been wiped out, rather amusing isn't it? But it just shows one how the German people are being kidded so as to keep up their spirits.

January 21 1915
Khartum

Dear Father,

Your very welcome letter of Dec 31 with the two £1 notes reached me by the last mail. They were very welcome; the day on which they arrived I had just drawn my last instalment of the previous money you sent from the bank, so forthwith I filled its place by putting 30/- in the bank, keeping 10/- in my box as pin money.

I told you in my last letter that I had joined the Signallers, it's awfully interesting. First of all we are learning the Semaphore method, after which comes the Morse system. Then next we shall start heliographing; by this latter method it is possible to send a message 70 miles providing you have an unobstructed view and a clear day, & it's done by means of the sun's rays acting on two ordinary mirrors, one being with the sender, the other with the receiver of the message. At night the same method is used, only by means of two lamps. This Signalling section also includes dispatch riding, & every morning we attend the lectures on the uses of a compass & geographical maps. It's like being at school again, only there is less sky-larking.

Last Sunday we were invited to the Palace. In parties of 20 we were shown round; it's a beautiful place & the gardens are magnificent. I'm sorry to say that when tea arrived some of the men made absolute pigs of themselves, so we cleared off to town. Actually two NCO's were caught pocketing buns with the result that some of the late arrivals for tea got none. It's very funny to think that such men as these are our seniors.

The other day I received a pair of socks & mittens from Ada Brooks; the socks will be very useful but I'm afraid there is not much use for mittens here as it's scorching hot even now, but all the same it's very thoughtful of them. You might thank them for me; of course I shall but at present I've no time. You will understand how much writing I've done when I tell you that the pad which Patty sent me at Xmas is now finished & I've only used it for letters.

Well, Father, I must finish now as I must do a bit of flag-wagging to prepare for the Exam. Remember me to Tom & Patty, not forgetting Lena, best love to Mother & yourself

I remain
Your Affectionate kid

PS What about the bombs dropped near London.

British Barracks, Khartum
Sudan
January 26 1915

Just a short line giving particulars of the PC I sent you. Baty, Smith, 2 Grangers, Frank Lomas & myself have applied for commissions. Staveacre & Smedley were consulted & they quite agreed with us. It's this way: I'm rather fed up with being a Tommy & if the War is going to be of long duration I don't like the idea of being a Private so long. Major Staveacre & Captain Smedley told us that they were wanting Officers for the Reserve Battalions in England, & also that we stood a very good chance. We have sent our letters of application, but of course we won't hear anything for a good time yet I don't suppose, as they have to be sent to the War Office in England. You have no idea how a Tommy is looked down upon by civilians. No matter who it is they are all classed the same, and it's not very nice for chaps like me who are used to something better, & ten-to-one could buy half of the high & mighty civilians up. Now don't let this worry you as we are all together & don't care a hang for anybody, but I know you will see my point. Awaiting your views on the matter.

British Barracks
Khartum
January 27th 1915

Dear Mother,

I have not much to tell you about, but I thought it would be as well to drop you a line to tell you that I'm in the best of health. I told you that I had received the pyjamas etc in a previous letter, & I had not any duty to pay. Katie & Lillie sent me a box of State Express Cigarettes for my birthday[†] & a week before I received a box from Doris Smith. The parcels you sent me for my birthday have not yet arrived, but I'm eagerly awaiting the same every day.

Just fancy, the end of January, and the temperature is 100°, so I'm making very good use of the print shirts you sent. On my birthday I had a game of billiards. I got back to the Mess about 6 o'clock & beheld my bed, decorated in a most unique fashion; the decoration consisted of my two flags across the back, & on the bed were all the old jam pots & tins that could be found.

I started my 23rd year well by going to the Cathedral at night; afterwards Baty, myself & a Regular from the Fort went to the Gardens & heard ''The Merry Widow'' & ''Little Grey Home in the West'' murdered by the native band. I kept my birthday up on Saturday by inviting about ten of the boys to the Canteen.

On Monday morning the Company didn't half go through it. They were marched onto the desert & had to dig a trench from 6am until 10.30am without breakfast. I can tell you, there wasn't half some grumbling about it; the poor chaps had got past their breakfast. Owing to Baty & myself being attached to the Signallers we don't dig trenches now, & I'm not sorry.

I am enclosing a few photographs taken by one or two chaps in the Mess. Have you seen the photos that Mr Barlow took of the Wedding Party? Janet sent me one, they are awfully good. Well I must close now as I'm going to do a bit of flag-wagging. Remember me to them all, not forgetting yourself.

I'm sorry to say that the happy party is being split up. The two Hollands, F Lomas, Denby, D Green & perhaps Herbert Smith are going on Monday to Atbara to relieve the troops who are at present there. It is a twelve hour's train journey from here, so I don't suppose we shall see them again until the journey home when we shall pick them up. H Smith is on the Reserve, so he might not go.

[†]24th January. He was 22.

British Barracks
Khartum
February 8th 1915
Monday

By the last mail I received twelve letters; apart from the papers you sent, seven of them were from home, the other five were from Beatrice, B Hamnett, K Smeeth, Patty & Tom, & much to my surprise & pleasure I got one from Mr Tom Plant, so I look like having a busy time for the next week or so, especially as I haven't yet answered all the previous mail. The mail is very irregular: there should be two a week, but before this last mail came in there had not been one for two weeks.

Last Monday I went to the so-called Theatre. It's the first time it's been opened since we arrived here & then it was only amateur. The Khartum Operatic Society assisted by Captain Smedley & Capt Norbury gave a little farce entitled "Eliza comes to Stay". It was very funny & I enjoyed it immensely. For the time being I forgot that I was in Khartum. The songs came in the nick of time, as the following night I was singing at the Institute, so I was able to give something fresh, having already given "Drake goes West" & "Lighterman Tom" about ten times.

The cake arrived last Monday in a beautiful condition; it wasn't the least bit dry & it's the best kind of cake you've made; in fact four of the boys were quite sick after eating one piece, but I'm pleased to say the my Little Mary† is quite agreeable to rich things, although it's very seldom it gets the chance of receiving them, but when it does it rises to the occasion & receives them in quite a hospitable manner. I haven't received Mrs Smith's cake yet, but am expecting it daily.

I wish you wouldn't send anything unless I ask for it. As you say, I do like to feel smart at times, but you forget that I'm in the Army & am not supposed to go out in anything but tunic, knickers, puttees & black boots. Shoes are not regimental; that's one thing which rubs me the wrong way; no matter what you have, you have to wear the regimental things so that everyone knows that you are a "Tommy", but all the same, when they arrive I shall do my best to use them, especially for when I go to church, as we go there in long trousers.

I think you have got rather an exaggerated idea of Eddie's friendship with Lieutenant Whitley. He has been to his room to tea once, but you must not forget that one is a Lieutenant & the other is a Private which is a large distinction in the Army. Even if you have a brother who is an Officer it would not be possible for him to go out with his brother, a Private, especially in these times as we are treated as Regular Soldiers. I must say that Lieutenant Whitley is the best Officer we have & always has a word for you on seeing you, but as far as going out with him, it's out of the question. Of course you needn't let this go any further.

†Little Mary - his stomach.

We've had a very busy week, a kind of Spring cleaning; one afternoon we cleared everything out of the Mess & set to work scrubbing the floors, window frames & mopping all the cobwebs off the walls & ceilings. Then another afternoon we scrubbed all the paint on the verandas. Although it was hard work we had quite a good time. The work being finished, a fierce fight ensued in which buckets & baths full of water took a prominent part. Of course on account of the heat, we had (practically speaking) no clothes on, so it was one way of having a showerbath. We were rewarded for our pains by the Colonel telling Captain Smedley that the Barrack Rooms of "D" Company were the cleanest in the Barracks.

I'm enclosing a few photographs of the various chaps in our Mess. You will see the chap who sleeps next to me now the Hollands have gone to Atbara, he is a Lance-Corporal & has the job of looking after the Company's rations, so I shouldn't go short, should I? He is an awfully decent chap. I've already sent you another cabinet of myself which I think does me justice at last, so I hope you will burn the other.

I must close now & get some of the other letters answered. By the way, I don't think I told you that I have now finished with the awful job of cleaning boots. I have entered into a contract with Babican (one of the blacks) to clean my boots every day, put my basin & plate on my shelf after washing & to run to the Canteen for me in a morning when I require anything, & he

does all this for the huge sum of $7\frac{1}{2}$d per week, which is a lot to him. I found Babican rather a mouthful so I've called him *Tom* after the Bury lad, & I rather think he likes his new name by the way he comes up on hearing it. Kind regards to Tom, Lena, Patty & everybody else.

I remain
Your Son
Jack

PS. I'm writing to Lena thanking her for the handkerchiefs. The photos I'm enclosing, put away so they won't get lost.

British Barracks
Khartum
February 13th 1915

Dear Father,

Although I've written Mother & Pat by this post I've still time to drop you a short line. I told you that F Lomas, Baty, H Smith two Grangers & myself had mentioned to Smedley & Staveacre about taking up Commissions, well since then things have moved very rapidly. Last Saturday the Colonel sent for us & said that he would recommend us as being quite capable of taking one up & last Tuesday we filled in our application forms which now will be on their way to England. I don't think I stand as much chance of getting one as the others because all of them have applied for either Kitchener's Army or the Territorials, whereas I have only applied for one in the Territorials, but according to what Capt Smedley told me the Terriers are wanting Officers, so I thought that I would have a shot ... am now awaiting the result. I might also tell you that before the papers were sent away we were examined and passed by the Doctor so that he could fill in the certificate that we were physically fit.

I'm enclosing a few photos taken by one of our chaps which you might take home and keep with the others I've sent. It tells you on the back what they are. Remember me to the ''Old War Horse'' (Mr Mercer), kind regards to any of the boys in the Houses who are still left.

To C.S.Morten, Earl of Arnwood
British Barracks
Khartum

Wed Feb 17 1915

Dear Father,

This is in reply to yours of Jan 29th which I have just received. You ask me whether we are going to France or not, well I cannot tell you as there are so many rumours floating around, but I don't think it will be before the end of the Summer & I sincerely hope that by next Christmas the War will be a thing of the past.

Re the Commissions I wrote about, since last time I wrote, things have moved very quickly. On Monday last the Sirdar interviewed us & I'm pleased to say that he has recommended us along with our Colonel. Of course the Sirdar is practically the King in this part of the world, & as the Sergeant-Major told us, his name on our papers is practically giving us a Commission. It's rather an honour being recommended by him, isn't it? I can tell you I was glad when the interview was over, as apart from the Sirdar, there were present three Officers on his staff, our Colonel & our Adjutant. As each one of us was interviewed they all stood round weighing up form as it were. Of course we had to stand perfectly rigid whilst he was talking to us. You won't half fancy your chance if I come back an Officer, will you, having gone out as a Private. NB On receipt of this letter, will you send immediately to the C.O. 7th Manchester Battalion, 99 Burlington Street, M/c a copy of my birth certificate. They must have it as early in March as possible ... I expect Mr Twyford will have a letter from the War Office as I had to give the address of the parson for a good character.

To Mrs Morten, Lady de Arnwood

British Barracks
Khartum
February 17 1915

Dear Mother,

Just a short line to tell you that I received the 10/- note which you so kindly sent & it's coming in very useful.

As you can see the photos are not good, but the one which is on the way you will find much better. It's all right you asking me to write to various people, but I'm fed up with writing, and have other things to do besides writing. I shall send Tandys a photo (not a letter) but I shall have to give old Kershaw a miss, you can tell Father to remember me to him. I received the cake from Mrs Smith, also a half-pound block of milk chocolate each for Baty, Eddy, Harold Herbert & myself, awfully good of them, isn't it? It was a tip-top cake in fact, nearly equal to your specials. I'm sorry to hear about Mrs Hardman and sincerely hope that the operation has been successful.

To Mrs Thomas Hardman (what is to be)

British Barracks
Khartum

Wed Feb 17 1915

Dear Pat,

Just a short letter. I'm so utterly fed up with writing that I'm cutting them all short & apart from this, it's costing me a fortune in stamps. Thanks awfully for your birthday present, but you haven't sent me a photo of *Mac* yet. I suppose Father has told you that there's a possibility of me coming back an Officer. I'm sorry to hear about Mrs Hardman. Tomorrow we are having another Lacrosse match. Hope Tom is better. I told you about receiving a photo from Barlows of the wedding, well I haven't yet replied as I haven't time, so tell Janet when you see her that I will write at the earliest opportunity.

Yours sincerely
Jack

Kind regards to all at Bury

February 24th
Wednesday

My Dear Mother,

I suppose by now you will have received my second photos. By your last letter you said that you were looking forward to one of my long letters, well I have quite made up my mind to curtail my letters as I'm so fed up with writing, but in your case I will make an exception, so here goes.

I'm still in the pink, in spite of having lost another pet. A short time ago I asked Friday to get me a dog, well last Thursday he presented me with one. I can't name the breed, but it resembled a ball of wool (there is no question about it being a mongrel) or else it was some thoroughbred specie peculiar to this country. In fact it was too young to have left its mother, it couldn't even lap, so for the short time I had it I fed it by means of soaking my thumb with Nestles milk & the dog sucked it. Thursday night it yelped all through the night & kept half the Mess awake. This state of affairs promised to continue all day Saturday & we were fairly sick of hearing it, so after puzzling my brain a happy idea struck me: why not put it with the she monkey we have in the Mess? I did this & left them. Going back in $\frac{1}{2}$ hour's time I discovered the monkey in the box with its paws round the dog, just as you would nurse a baby. Here I had further difficulties; no matter what I or any of the others did the monkey would not let us even go near the dog, & as for touching it, well it was quite out of the question, & the dog was quite happy, in fact you couldn't separate the two. Friday afternoon I thought I would examine my hound, & much to my sorrow I found it was alive with insects nearly as big as the dog itself, so after the owner of Chico (the monkey) had taken it away in fearful haste, I handed Friday the dog with instructions not to bring it back until it was at least two months old & thoroughly clean, then I would inspect it. Up to writing I have not quite made up my mind what animal to go in for in the meantime.

Last Sunday we had a surprise: the Daily News people sent the Battalion a number of Xmas puddings. It panned out at $^{1}/_{2}$ a pound a man which we had on Sunday, & I must say I've never tasted a nicer pudding, not even at home. It was a rare surprise.

The Egyptian ADC

Sunday night I had the real 1st night out I've had since arriving here. The Egyptian A.D.C. to the Sirdar invited Baty, Eddy, Harold, Smith, Lomas & myself to his house for supper. We all went except Harold & Lomas who are I'm sorry to say in hospital, & Eddy who has a bad leg, but not in hospital. The three of us had a ripping time, & managed very well to sneak past the sentries on arriving back at Barracks about 12 o'clock. I felt more at home than I have for six months, although it was rather strange to see decent table linen and drink out of dainty tea-cups.

By the way, this applies to all of you at home, don't repeat yourselves so much in your letters. For instance you've told me in twelve letters that Mrs S- is sending me a cake. In a case like that one is apt to think that twelve cakes are coming, & apart from from this it's awfully annoying on opening letters, instead of fresh *news* you find yourself reading something which you read a month ago. I hope you will excuse these caustic remarks, but I'm in one of my telling-off moods. I should also appreciate a little more information about Father's new Agency.

I'm sorry to hear about Mrs Hardman & trust that the operation has been successful. It was a most thoughtless move to get without Mac. Who will now take Patty for a walk in the middle of the week? She'll pine her little heart away, unless Tom happens to have a another *serious* attack during one of his week-end visits to Arnwood.

Immediately on receipt of this will you tell Mr Twyford that he will receive a letter direct from the War Office with regards to my character. Incidentally, Father might possibly stand him a drink at my expense (it goes a long way at times, you know). Putting all kid on one side, you will tell Mr Twyford, won't you? Tomorrow my Exam comes off so I will now close.

British Barracks
Khartum
February 28 1915

Dear Mr & Mrs Morten,

I was pleased to hear from Jack that you approved of our latest spasm in the Military line, it's the first step towards being a Field Marshall if it comes off, and my people expressed a wish that we should come back at least Generals, so we thought we had better start right away.

You will be pleased to hear that Jack looks a picture of health but he's getting quite fat, in fact we are all putting on flesh. Harold was in hospital for a few days last week but it was only slight throat trouble and he is quite alright again; my own private opinion is that he likes getting there and knows how to do the trick – you see, they get chicken and all sorts of good things to eat, and he was always fond of Little Mary. We get very little news from the fellows in the 6th Battalion now at Cairo, but they appear to be having a good time judging by their letters to the Guardian & Echo.

Has Jack told you about his dogs? He suddenly got an idea into his head to keep a dog and by mysterious methods of his own, got hold of an awful little specimen. It did not take us long to point out to him that it was rather alive and grubby, so he very reluctantly parted with it. His second venture was rather better; my surprise was great when I came in to find him feeding a worried looking puppy about 8 weeks old. This one seemed quite clean and looked like being a success until we got to bed. I think we had been asleep about an hour when the whole Mess were startled to hear terrible howls from the veranda. It was Jack's dog crying for Mother, and it seemed very obstinate about it too – we only got peace and quietness when someone put a bath over it. I am sorry to say the dog has disappeared. Meanwhile we are waiting for his final venture in the dog line, but perhaps it will be a monkey, they are better to keep than dogs out here.

I am sending you a photograph of myself. I may as well tell you that I nearly drove the photographer mad before he gave me satisfaction and I conceited enough to think that it's rather good (for Khartoum)

Trusting that you are all well, Tom included

With kindest regards
Yours sincerely
Edgar Granger

I might almost venture to send my love to Pattie. I don't think you can reach me here.

The British Barracks
Khartum
Monday March 1st 1915

Dear Pat,

Thanks for your letter of 1st Feb; as you say they are short but sweet. I have received the letter from Mother in which Father adds a little note saying how pleased he is that I have gone in for a commission, & I must say it relieved my mind somewhat as I didn't quite know how he would receive the news, knowing his whims and moods as you know them. Of course if he had cultivated a boil or had been suffering from one of his indigestion bouts, there is no telling how he would have taken it, but from the tone of his letters I'm pleased to say he appears to be in the pink, although with the manager of Turtle House being so far away he will have double anxiety on his shoulders, but there you see again "An active mind makes a man young".

Talking about these commissions, I think we stand an extremely good chance, as apart from the Sirdar signing the papers, I was told today on very good authority, that he also wrote a personal letter recommending us.

I received the packet of Gold Flake from Mother & I think it is a jolly good idea of hers sending these little packets every so often, in fact quite a nice steady income, because out here we all smoke about twice the amount we do at home. I think it's an outrage, that now the Government make us pay duty on eatables & cigarettes; of course up to now I've been lucky as I got all the Xmas & Birthday tit-bits before this new regulation came into force, & the 100 cigs Mother sent by post were not opened by the Censor, but Eddy & one or two other fellows have had to pay quite a lot on things. In my opinion it comes to this: that for serving the Government they pay you with one hand and take it off you with the other, so if you happen to be sending out anything in the shape of parkin etc, you had better send them duty-paid; of course for little parcels by letter post, as you send the cigs, it does not matter.

No doubt you will be pleased to hear that I have passed my Signalling Exam. The Examiner was a Captain in the Coldstream Guards, a beastly knut, but an awfully decent fellow.

Eddy has written to Mother & Father by this mail and told them about my second attempt at keeping a dog, so I will not bore you with it. Mr Hallowell sent me a box of 200 cigarettes. They were about the best mild cigarettes I've had, jolly sporty of him. wasn't it?

I felt quite a knut last night as I went to the Cathedral in the brown shoes. I have bought three "Ostrich Feathers" & am sending them home to you. I bought them on account of their cheapness, namely 3d each. Let me know how they suit & if it is worth you having them curled at home, because if so I can send you any amount. As far as my knowledge extends I think you will find them much cheaper than you can buy them at home. I quite agree with you about *W.S.* & thank you for the "Motherly Advice". Mother says she would like a photo of me with the monkey; well I haven't got one, but will have it taken again. I must close now, best love to Father, Mother, Lena & yourself. Kind regards to all at Davenport Park.

PS In the signalling exam I passed 1st Class in the reading of messages with 98%. In the sending I passed 2nd Class with 97%. It is awfully rotten luck; if I had got 1% more in the sending I should have got 1st Class for both, but it's not so dusty when you take into consideration that some of the fellows who have been signalling for years only got 2nd Class in both.

The sardines packed in the shoes were jolly good.

British Barracks
Khartum
Monday March 8th

Dear Old Pat,

You are really an old sport for keeping me so well informed about things, it's the only thing we have to look forward to, that is when the mail arrives which is very erratic. There is supposed to be an English mail on Thursdays & Sundays, but it's nothing at all extraordinary to be told that it has missed the train to Cairo, & sometimes there is a lapse of twelve days from one mail to another.

By the last mail I received 150 cigarettes from Dick (the 2nd lot he has sent me) also a letter from he & Marion in which he stated that Marion was sending me some chocolate, jolly decent of them, isn't it? This is what I call a real Pal. He has been to the Isle of Man this winter for his health & he says he is thinking about joining the Army A.S.C. He is just the chap for the job being able to handle a motor like he does. I don't know whether I have told you, but I had a letter about three months ago from a chap Eddy & myself met at Port Erin, by the way a Jew, but an awfully decent fellow. In this letter he said it would give him real pleasure to send us anything we required, so of course Eddy & myself like to give anybody real pleasure when we can, so one night we concocted a masterpiece in writing. Eddy wrote it & I composed it & in a very nice way we told him that decent Virginia cigs could not be bought out here, & I'm pleased to say that out efforts have been rewarded. By the last mail we received a letter from him in which he informed us that he had sent us each a box of Abdullah Virginia Cigs. There is nothing like that old saying that "an opportunity missed is an opportunity lost" & Eddy & myself always bear that in mind. I might say that we did it for devilment more than anything else, just to test the chap, & I think you will agree with us that he is a ripping fellow.

The Signallers have had a group taken including the Adjutant & Colonel & it's turned out jolly well. I've ordered a large one which I will send home in about a week's time. It cost me 5/- but it's worth it as apart from making a good picture, it will be something to look at when I'm old & grey, which by the way won't be very long if I stay out here many more months. I'm sorry to say that there is some talk of disbanding the Signallers, I hope it does not come to anything as it's been an absolute birthday ever since we joined, besides being very interesting. The other morning the Company paraded from 5 o'clock in the morning until 11.30, whereas we Signallers had our usual parade from 6 till 8. Baty & I really enjoyed lying in bed watching Eddy & the others parade out at 5 o'clock, & of course if we disband it will mean us going back to Company Drill.

I remain
Yours fed up
Jack

Some of the boys here had word from home not to stamp their letters. Let me know at once if this is allright, because it will save a lot of money.

The British Barracks
Khartum
Monday March 8th 1915

Dear Mother,

This is in reply to yours of Feb 15th. The mail at this end is very irregular, of course you know there are two ways by which it comes, one is the long sea route & the other overland which only takes about 18 days. One week I get letters from you of a previous date to the ones I got the week before; I suppose it is something similar at your end.

There is not much news to relate, but I must not forget to mention that they are at last beginning to feed us like human beings. Now that the very hot weather has made its presence felt our meals have been altered to suit it. We have breakfast about 9 o'clock (every morning liver & onions varied once in every seven days with porridge), after this we fast until 6 o'clock in the evening except for a pint of tea which we have at 1 o'clock noon. We have now been on this diet for a week & it is a decided improvement, as it gives the cooks (who by the way are a fresh lot) plenty of time for cooking it well and thereby making it tender. I am now recovering from a good meal, as tonight we had roast beef, beans and potatoes followed by macaroni pudding. You see with this new idea, instead of the Company's ration money going in buying tinned stuff for tea (such as herrings which are very dear and not at all palatable) it is spent on more substantial things such as beans potatoes & pudding. You may think it's bad management, we being out here five months before such a beneficial move should be tried, but it's a way the Army have got.

I expect now you will have received my new photograph. Last night Baty & myself went to the Cathedral; Captain Smedley sang the solo in the Anthem; he's a most cultivated voice. I will now close as I'm endeavouring to write to Father & Patty by this mail if time permits.

Tuesday March 9th 1915

Dear Father,

This is in reply to yours of Feb 19th. I have not much to say as I suppose you will read Pattie's & Mother's letters. I received the papers you sent. I'm glad you are sending Chambers as the serials are very good, but up to now I'm fed up with reading papers as there is nothing in them except that the Allies have captured a trench and advanced a few yards & at the rate they have been going it will take them a deuce of a time to go a long way, but now Spring has arrived I'm hoping for more decisive results.

I don't like your silence with regard to business, you might let me know if there is anything or nothing doing, & if we are likely to recover after the War. How are the rents coming in? and by the way, how about Jackonette?

I'm more than pleased to hear that you agreed with my action re Commission. I expect we shall hear in a week or so, & I'm inclined to think that we shall get them. Kind regards to Mr Mercer.

PS I'm enclosing a page out of Chamber's Journal. It's new to me there being some fine Celluloid works in Finland.

Khartum
Wednesday March 17 1915

Yours & Father's letter from Llandudno to hand. I was surprised to hear of you being there, but am glad to see that you don't let these hard times interfere with your annual pick-me-up.

We have heard about the Commission, in fact they are practically fixed up. We are expecting a cable at any moment instructing us where to go, & we fully expect that this week we shall leave Khartum, but where to I cannot yet tell, however as soon as we know I will let you have a cable. Don't be a bit surprised if this time next month I'm telling you verbally my experiences out here. In any case don't send off any more parcels until you hear from me again.

The heat is absolutely unbearable. I'm sorry to say that Jack Thorpe is very seriously ill, & I don't expect that we shall see him in Khartum any more; you know that when he got better from his attack of dysentery he went to Wadi Halfa acting as Censor and whilst he has been there he has had a very bad attack; I've forgotten the name of the ailment, but it seriously affects the heart, & I believe he has been invalided to Cairo.

I also regret to inform you that Major Hertz (one of the very best) has been invalided home to England. Whilst out here he was operated on for Appendicitis; the operation proved very successful and whilst he was in the convalescent stage the poor chap was stung in the eyes by an insect making him partially blind; however there is every hope that he will regain his sight, but everyone of us in the Battalion regret that he has had to go home, as there is no Officer in the Battalion who is so energetic in arranging competitions, concerts etc for the men in their spare time as he was, & in a desolated spot like this a man like this is essential to the troops.

Tomorrow the races are on, so if the expected cable does not come I shall be at my usual post in the judges box, on the other hand if it does, I shall either be amongst the knuts or else in the Officer's Mess.

Khartum
Wednesday March 24 1915

This is in reply to Mother's letter written at Mrs Fletcher's & Father's letter of the 5th. To tell the truth I'm nearly falling asleep whilst writing as I've been a long walk today, but as the mail goes tomorrow & I've a few others to write I haven't any time for sleeping; then of course where duty comes in a *soldier* never sleeps. I think I have a perfect right to call myself a soldier after what I have gone through in the last six months.

As you know the Blue Nile runs along the Barracks & I've been along it dozens of times. The White Nile runs about three miles west of the Barracks, so today being a whole holiday, Baty, Lomas, Manning & myself decided to explore its banks. I'm sorry to say we had to go without Baty as he was collared for onion-peeling. The three of us started soon after breakfast on donkeys as far as the White Nile. Here we dismounted, paid the donkey boys after some excited talk about Backsheesh, which is Arabic for tips. The natives are terrors for backsheesh. If you only say *Saida* which means "How do you do", they ask you for backsheesh. Of course, needless to say, they don't get much out of me.

Proceeding on with the walk, we now walked for about five miles along the banks & it was a real surprise for me the whole way along: both banks were very thickly cultivated with beans, cabbages, potatoes etc, & the most charming part of it was the nice springy grass which we walked along, a real treat after having trodden on nothing but sand for six months. We nearly fancied that we were on the Welsh hills, but this was not to extend very far as you will presently see. Of course, as you no doubt know, the soil is so fertile on these banks that they can get four crops a year. After going a little further we branched off & came once more to barren desert.

It now being 12.30 our little Mary's began speaking, so seeing a few trees a little distance away we made for them in order to sit down in the shade and partake of our frugal lunch. Here again we were reminded of the awful country we were in, as we found out that the flies which are absolutely a curse here also liked the shady trees, so in the end we had to sit in the open under a blazing sun & have our lunch. The sand was so scorched that before sitting down we had to lay our tunics on it, & as soon as the sardines (which I received from you on Monday) were opened, we were pestered even here with the flies & the water in our bottles was so warm that to quench our thirst we simply swilled our mouths with it. Having eaten our food as quickly as possible we started for the homeward journey across the desert. I've read about bleached bones on the desert, well today I've seen plenty of them. One little patch of about $1/2$ mile square was covered with nothing but the framework of cows, camels, goats etc, all the flesh having been eaten off them. Here we also saw a couple of huge Vultures looking for any tasty bits which might have been left on these beasts. You've heard me speak of the desert dogs, well these & the Kite Hawks which are very numerous in the Sudan, are the scavengers which nature has very thoughtfully placed here, & anyone found shooting them is liable to a very heavy fine, as without these scavengers the place would be overrun with disease. We got back about three o'clock, & although after our trying task we were wet through with perspiration, we have come to the conclusion that when possible it is far better than sticking & moping in the Barracks, so you will see that today I have earned a good night's sleep.

Tomorrow we are having a field day along with the Gypos & Sudanese. Reveille goes at 4 o'clock AM.

The sponge roll & the soda cake were in a beautiful & moist condition; by the way I prefer the soda cake out here to the rich one as it goes further & fills up more corners. I'm pleased to hear that you have sent me some more money. I hope it lands this week as I'm once again verging on bankruptcy, not having a single piastre until Friday which is pay day.

Much to my surprise we are still here, but have been living on the hope for a week now that on the morrow the expected cable would come telling us that we had got our Commissions. I'll let you know by cable as soon as we hear.

PS Have got no stamps, so am sending this without. I believe the Authorities pass them. Let me know.

Khartum
March 29 1915

This is in reply to yours of the 11th & 12th which I received yesterday. The 30/- came just at the right moment.

As you will see by the heading I'm still rotting away in Khartum, but each day all of us have presentiments that we shall hear something on the morrow. As you know Baty & I are now back with the Company, having passed the Signalling Exam we only parade with them occasionally now. The great drawback to being back with the Company is that we have to do our share of Guards but I can't grumble as I've only done two this year up to now, & don't expect I shall have the opportunity of doing many more if things turn up as we expect.

Last Friday, along with Eddy & Harold I was put on the Quarter Guard, but when the Officer inspected us before going on, he picked me out for the stick; so as you know I didn't do any Sentry Gd, but looked after the Guard's meals & so had my usual night's slumber in my bed.

A rather strange thing happened: whilst I was away getting the Guards some biscuits, they caught & killed a snake about three feet long, just as it was entering the Guard Room. It looked quite a harmless creature, it was so beautifully spotted, but I fancy if I had seen it alive I should have looked at it in quite a different light; I know that I shouldn't have had much sleep with the thought that at any moment one might crawl over me, so I was very fortunate in getting the stick in more senses than one.

I'm sorry to hear that the Belgian Agency is a fiasco; do try someone else without the help of Hupfeld; of course if he can put anything good in our way I know you will take advantage of it, but I should be much more at ease if you could snap something up on your own, so that in future we can do business without Turtle House, *London* making money from our energy & enterprise. I hope the new collar will be a success.

Last Saturday a concert was held when I rendered ''Long ago in Alcala'' to a very appreciative audience & was encored. I will drop F. Butler a PC. He'll be rather surprised to hear from me in this outlandish region.

You say you are trying to get fleecy goods from America; I hope you succeed & if you can manage to get it direct, don't fiddle about with their M/c representatives, because you know, 1% is 1%. I suppose that I have quite a substantial banking account now.

Before closing I might say that just outside the Barracks on the Desert there is an anti-aircraft gun & it's most interesting when they are practising to see the shrapnel shells bursting in the air. "Belle Vue" isn't in it. I don't know what the idea is in having one here, as there is not much to attract any daring German Aviator here; in fact there is nothing but a very hot reception from the lads of the 7th Manchesters. I am now absolutely drained of all the news so will close.

Easter Monday
April 5th 1915

Dear Pat,

Who would have thought that on Easter Monday night I should be writing here whilst you are dancing & *sitting out* on the stairs of the Craig-y-Don.

Talking about B_ M_ saving money, I'm not surprised to hear how much he has sent home, as I've never seen him spend a $1/2$ piastre yet, & I would not sit & moapse† (sic) about like he does for a pension; it would drive me crazy; it's quite bad enough without making yourself miserable.

I'm sorry to hear that Father has again started the boil craze; I expect he has been feeding too well & I shall most certainly tell him off when I come back; of course I expect he knows the old remedy with a bottle; it's rather severe but most effective & there is nothing like the old remedies.

Tom will have a good time at Llandudno playing golf with the young budding lawyer, whilst you & his buxom sister go picking up on the pier, you know who I mean B_ & N_.

I'm sorry I have not a photo left, but next time I am taken I will let you have one. In the meantime you can adorn your bedroom with one of the two which I have already sent. Thanks very much for the 5/-. I've spent it on a dinner & a good selection of postcards.

I've just been cursing Baty: I got a horrid fly in my eye, so he came to the rescue & in trying to extricate it put his finger in my eye, but in the end he managed it.

Yesterday, being Easter Sunday, at night, Baty & I went to the Cathedral, afterwards proceeding to a cafe in town where our band was playing. I'm sending a PC to Frank Butler. By the way, you might tell me who he is struck on this Easter, don't forget, also tell me if Miss Blue & party are there again. It's awfully sad about Tom Sutton; one of the boys had a

Stockport Echo sent and I saw his photograph in it. I have received Mother's letter of the 17th ulto.

Harold is now out of hospital, but I'm sorry to say that my next-but-one companion, Walter Manning was taken into the hospital last Saturday with a slight attack of Malaria; of course, don't spread it around Davenport. I've also received Father's letter of 19 ulto & the papers.

You would have a night of scandal when Granny Slack came round. I can just see you sat in the corner trying to get a word in; I bet you found your match at talking.

As you will see by the address we are still at Khartum, but I feel sure we shall hear something this week. The other night there was a parade trench digging, well it happened that Eddy & I were orderlies for the week & we didn't feel keen on trench-digging, so we squared the Orderly Corporal (my bed-mate) to find us a job of peeling potatoes. We had finished this job by 8 o'clock, so went back to the Mess & got into our pyjamas & sat talking. The Company arrived back at 9 o'clock & Smedley saw us in our pyjamas. As it happens the Colonel had given orders that every available man had to be on parade, so on Saturday we were up before Smedley when he chalked us off & remanded us until tomorrow, but I think it will blow over as he has gone with a party to inspect the cotton growing district up the Nile.

Tell Lena she is a jolly good old sport, & the cigs came duty-free, but I'll write & thank her myself. I will close now, hoping you had a good time at Llandudno and that you are all in the pink after your Easter holiday. Best love to all.

Khartum
Saturday April 10 1915

Just a few lines to tell you I'm in the pink.

Yesterday we got some good news. We are moving from Khartum with the Battalion next week. The first half go on Wednesday & we are being amongst the second half on Friday. One of the London City Battalions are relieving us here. I don't know yet where our destination is, all we do know is that there is a steamer waiting for us at Port Sudan. One rumour is that we are going either to Cairo or Alexandria for a short time, then on to the Dardanelles; then another rumour is that we are coming to England for a month or two, then going to France. Of the two I prefer the latter, but I'll let you know all particulars as soon as possible.

Up to writing we've heard nothing further about our Commissions, but are still hoping.

There's any amount of work to be done now, packing things up & loading carts etc with all the stores of the Battalion, so I'll have to close. Hoping to see you very soon.

I remain
Your Son
Jack

PS By the enclosed photo you will see the size of the snake we killed.

Khartum
Wednesday Apri.' 14 1915

By the last letter I sent you will naturally come to the conclusion that I'm far away from this awful place by now, but I'm sorry to say that we are still roasting here.

Yesterday we were packed up all ready for going but it's just like we were at Littleboro. We are expecting to go any day and the sooner we get word the better. Moving away from a place in the Army is a thousand times more trouble than you can possibly realise until you've gone through it; it's a jolly good thing that we don't move so often. All this week we've been sleeping without any sheets, blankets & biscuits (Army phrase for mattresses) & take my word for it that an iron bed without any of these is not too comfortable. Of course I'm better off than some of the boys as I've got plenty of flesh on my bones. This is another reason why I don't envy a long stay in Khartum, because now these comforts have gone into the Stores, the longer we are here the longer we will have to sleep on iron beds.

I was nearly roasted this morning: from 10 o'clock until 1 o'clock I was loading transport carts with ammunition, blankets, provisions etc ready for the journey. Of course under ordinary conditions we are not supposed to leave the Barrack Room for any length of time between the hours of 9 o'clock & 5 o'clock as the heat is so terrific.

One of the hardest jobs I've had was to get all my things into one kit-bag. It's really a work of art how I've managed; needless to say I couldn't possibly manage to squeeze any curios in. I can't say yet where our destination is; all that we know is that we are embarking at Port Sudan for Port Suez, & from there we are going to Cairo to join the Division, then after a short stay we shall all move together, where to I don't know.

Yesterday morning the Sirdar reviewed us & one of the Battalions in the Egyptian Army presented us with its Colours, so when the time comes we won't half swank[†] marching down Market Street[‡] with these Colours. In saying Goodbye the Sirdar complimented us on our general military bearing & said that we were equal to any Regulars.

[†]swank - show off.

[‡]Market Street - Manchester's main shopping street. These colours were presented to the Ladysmith Barracks in Ashton. Later they were transferred to the Regiment Museum, then in November 1945 to Manchester Cathedral where they were laid up. They can still be seen there.

I had a lovely cup of tea yesterday: One of our Officers, Lieut. Brown invited Eddy, Harold & myself to his room. It was quite a treat having tea with milk in it.

I'm sorry to say that we are still patiently waiting to hear of our Commissions; that's one thing you *have* to learn in the Army (patience). I'm a little bit dubious myself, but all our Officers think that we shall get them.

Abbassia Barracks, Cairo
Wednesday April 21 1915

At last we have left Khartum. The Battalion left in two parts, the first half left last Friday & the second last Sunday. I & the boys were with the first lot, and it was a journey; for making a general mess & mismanagement the 7th take the cake every time.

As you know the journey from Khartum to Port Sudan is 750 miles & we were packed like herrings in a box, so what with the tropical weather & the packing we had a fairly hot time. About 9 o'clock I got down on the floor & managed to have a good night's sleep. There is nothing like adapting oneself to the circumstances. The next morning we stopped at Masma for breakfast. Here we all got out of the train & lined up on the station when we were dished out with bully beef & tinned salmon. There was supposed to be a pint of tea for each man, but the usual 7th mismanagement occurred and we only had a gill.

We arrived at Port Sudan about 7.30 on Saturday evening the 17th where we bivouacked on the open desert for the night. Of course you know the whole time we have had a detachment at Port Sudan, & among them was Joe Chatterton, so I slept in his tent for the night. It's a marvel to me that all the fellows were not laid up with cold, owing to the difference from the dry climate of Khartum. At Port Sudan the dew is so heavy that in the morning our rifles were red rusty, & the shirts which we had taken off and put on the ground beside us for the night were wet through, so I consider I was jolly lucky being asked in a tent.

The next day was Sunday & we were finnicking† (ask Father if this is the right way to spell it) about the whole day. We were due on the boat at 10 o'clock, but it was in such a filthy condition that Major Staveacre refused to take it over until they had cleaned it. We embarked about 4 o'clock in the afternoon & even then the boat was dirty, so from getting on to getting off we spent the whole time swabbing the decks. Our second party arrived on Tuesday 20th & we set sail the same night. I might say that F.Lomas, Baty & myself were orderlies for the voyage so we escaped all the fatigues for loading the boat & also the deck swabbing. All we had to do was look after the meals for our mess, keep it clean & wash their pots after each meal. In other words we were scullery maids. We only had two towels, one for washing the other for drying, and towards the end of the voyage the towels put more grease on the pots than they took off, talk about pigging it.

The boat was the White Star liner "The Suvic". I don't know whether you recollect but some years ago it split right in two parts. However they've patched it up & it's now used as a horse boat. It was very funny, half of the men had to sleep in the horse stalls. In spite of these petty trials, it was a jolly sight more comfortable than being on the Grantully Castle, & I wouldn't have cared a hang if we had been on it for six months, but no such luck. It was simply a two days voyage, you may think it was funny that our Officers made us clean the boat so thoroughly for such a short voyage, but nobody knew, not even the Colonel, where we were bound for. We were under sealed orders as far as Port Suez.

We arrived there on the Friday about 8 o'clock in the morning; here we got orders to disembark which we did about 2 o'clock. We now entrained for Cairo, which is an 8 hours run. The train journey was far more interesting than the journey from Khartum to Port Sudan. The railway runs along the side of the Suez Canal, and as you know, all along the banks are trenches, and the 33rd Punjabis (Indian Regt) are here on outpost duty. At one or two stations where we stopped we got into conversation with some of them and they are a very fine lot. The latter part of the journey was very similar to a train ride through the country at home, & it was a delightful change to see stretches of green fields instead of the bare sand.

We arrived at Cairo at 8.30 pm and alighted right at the entrance to the Barracks, but we weren't so near as we thought, as where we are camped is about a mile and a half from the entrance. We are away from everyone next to the Australians. I've only been here a day and I'm already fed up with Cairo, and long for the comforts of Khartum. After being in such Barracks for 7 months, camp life doesn't go down very well.

The 6th Manchesters are in the Barracks about half an hours walk from our camp, so yesterday morning I walked down to see them. It was like being at home again. They were all there, Heydons, Listers, Vernon Firth, Stanley Cragg, Bleakley and a chap Philip Biggs and an old pal of mine from Barlow & Jones, and tons of others, I can't name them all. They asked me to stay for dinner, so I dined with Edgar Lomas, Stanley Cragg, Bleakley & Vernon

†Finnicking about - wasting time.

Firth. After dinner we went on talking so I stayed to tea. When I got back to camp at night I discovered that our Company did not get dinner until 4 o'clock and then it wasn't fit to eat, so I was glad I stayed with the Sixth. It was the best dinner I've had in the Army. It's now 3.30 & our dinner isn't ready yet, so if things don't alter I can see myself living on the hospitality of the 6th. The weather here is very different from Khartum. The boys who have been here all along were complaining of the heat, whereas it was just right for we chaps, and up to now we've had our greatcoats on at night.

The tobacco that Tom sent & the 1 pound note arrived a day before we left Khartum, very lucky wasn't it? I'm writing to Tom when we are settled down; I shall have more time then. Owing to the Australians behaving like lunatics in town we are all confined to the Barracks, but a certain percentage of us can get a pass for certain days, so I expect I shall have a bit of sightseeing for a week or so. I've not been in town yet as I've been kept pretty busy visiting pals in the various Battalions.

I'm writing this under difficulties having no table, not even a box, and the Corporal of our tent has got a visitor who is three sheets in the wind & he is making us die with laughter.

I'm sorry to say there is no Khedives pay here, so I'll have to try to exist on 32 piastres a week (or in other words 1/- a day), of course eatables are much cheaper here than in Khartum, but I shall spend the extra money in sightseeing. I'm not in the same tent as the Grangers, Hollands & Baty, but I'm in the next with H Smith, Moss & Powell & Walter Manning; of course we're all together in the daytime. Eddy was very bad with heat stroke on the way down here, but I'm pleased to say he is alright now. There is a rumour that we are all coming home next month but I don't attach any importance to it as we get startling rumours every day. I will close now. We've heard nothing more about the commisions

---

Cairo
May 1 1915

This is in reply to yours of April 3rd & 9th which I received this week. In reply to your question about the Exam, I did a little better than Marshall. You will have received my first letter from here & I expect this will be the last I shall write from Cairo. Things are moving very rapidly. We've been here just a week & already the order has come through to move, in fact the whole Division are moving, they were simply waiting for our Battalion. We don't know much but it is rumoured that we move this next week.

First of all we are going to Mex (about 16 miles from Alexandria) & from there I can't say where we are bound for. At last we are being dished out with a full kit, so it is quite evident that a long journey is before us when the Battalion start to give us clothing etc. I shan't be sorry to leave Cairo as it's a dirty place, even in the centre of town it reeks, & the ground where we are encamped is so *lousy* that some of the fellows are covered with bites. I must be rather tough as last night was the first time they bothered me.

The other day we caught a 3ft snake crawling under the flap of the tent, so we all made a dashing bayonet charge & killed it. You've heard me talk about flies in Khartum, well without any exaggeration they are a million times worse here. We feed in small wooden sheds & practically every time we go for a meal we can't see the top of the table for flies, they're absolutely chronic.

The other night the Brigade had a full pack route march of 15 miles, & they actually ordered we chaps from Khartum to go. It was rather a tall order for us considering that we have never had any marching with full pack, but we did it & were as fit as ever at Reveille next morning. I had a pair of boots 1 size too large as I had no others, so I put a pair of socks in & wore two pairs on my feet with plenty of boracic acid in them, & when I arrived back, before getting down to sleep I washed them in cold water & they haven't bothered me a bit.

Tomorrow I'm going to see the Pyramids & the Sphinx & in the evening having a walk round the town. Since arriving here I've been down to the Sixth Barracks every night. I'm enclosing a couple of PC's, I've got quite a number which I will send as soon as I have time to parcel them up. Tell Pat that the Ostrich Feathers were a bad egg.

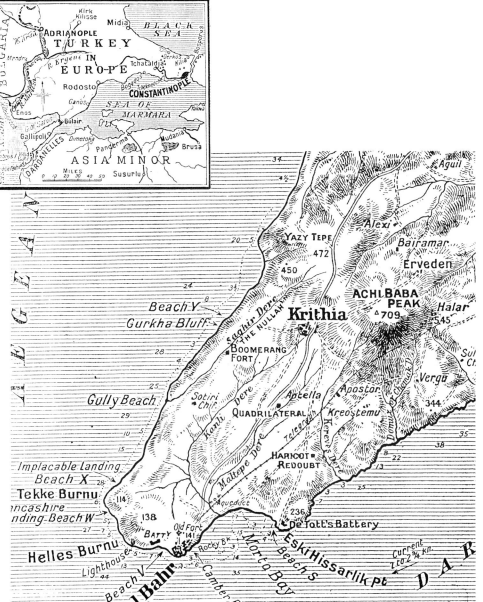

GALLIPOLI

Sunday May 8 1915

Dear Father,

I'm writing this in a dug-out on the Gallipoli Peninsular. I expect you got my PC from Alexandria, well I spent the whole day looking round & we sailed about 8 o'clock at night, down the Mediterranean & into the Gulf of Saros which we reached on Thursday.

On Friday night we landed on the Peninsular[†] & marched straight away to where we now are. We bivouacked for the night & next morning we made a dug-out for ourselves. There are two of us in my little shanty, a fellow named Brockbank & myself & we are as snug as a bug in a rug.

Yesterday a terrific battle took place, the whole day through nothing but the roaring of guns could be heard, & by Jove, they don't half roar; what with our guns behind firing over us & the ones in front, it's like a terrific thunderstorm. I can tell you the last two days must have been like Hell to the Turks. A few of their shells dropped over

[†]They landed on V beach, Cape Helles.

us, but the only damage done was that Barratt got a small piece if shrapnel in his *stern*, it was so slight that immediately afterwards he was walking about as usual. So long as we keep in our dug-outs when the enemy's shells are about (which is not very frequent) we are as safe as eggs, & the Turks are in full retreat. We are here as a Reserve, the Sixth boys lines are just in front of ours, so we are all together again. I could give you a much longer & more descriptive version but I don't think it would be allowed to go through, in fact I'm not quite certain whether this will be passed but I'm writing it on the off chance.

I had a very good breakfast of bacon which I cooked & bully beef, & my partner is now preparing the dinner. I'm in the pink of condition & absolutely settled down to my new home. There is nothing to worry about as we're quite happy & the two of us work together A1.

I don't suppose I shall be able to write quite so regularly as I did from Khartum owing to any difficulties in the transport which sometimes arise on these occasions, but I will write as often as possible, if is only a PC. Of course money is no good here, but I expect they will deliver parcels to us; so anything in the nature of cocoa & something to eat will be an agreeable change. Give my best love to Mother, Patty, Lena & Tom & remember me to the usual crowd. Hoping you are as well as I am.

I remain, Your affectionate Son
Jack

PS I don't think I would mention anything to Barratt's Father about him being wounded unless he mentions it.

Monday May 17 1915

Dear Father,

Just a line to let you know that I'm in the pink. I received your letter in which you enclosed an introduction to Mr Del Sandys, but I'm sorry I shall not be able to take advantage of it having left Khartum four weeks ago. For the last week I've been in the trenches & have now come back to our dug-outs for a very welcome rest. When I've time I'll write you a longer letter, also I'll write Tom & Pat. Remember me to them. My address is

The Mediterranean Expeditionary Force

A few cigs will be very welcome.

Wednesday June 2nd 1915

I'm fairly in the thick of it now, but there is no earthly reason for you to worry yourselves about me, & if you can't read some of the words, don't get excited & talk about sending me to a writing school when I return, because really in my opinion I'm doing a most clever thing; in order to shade myself from the burning sun whilst writing this, I'm lying down in the trench on my back with my knees upright to form a writing pad.

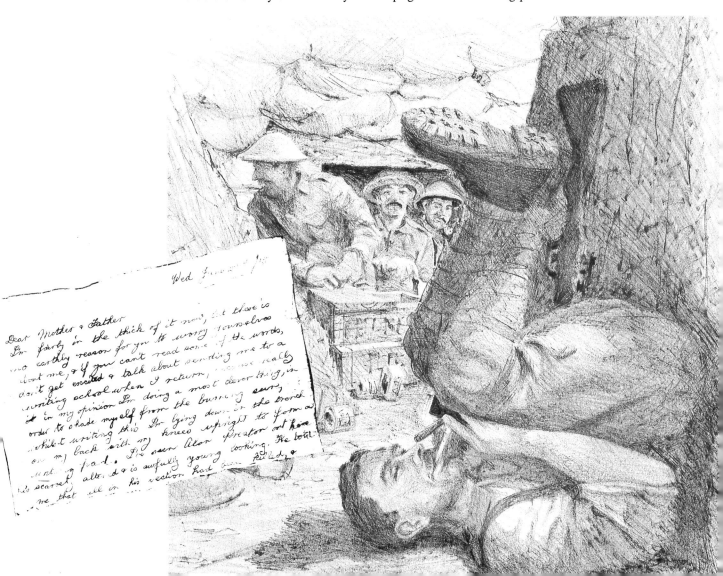

I've seen Alan Preston out here, he's scarcely altered & is awfully young looking. He told me that all in his section had been killed & amidst heavy shrapnel fire he stuck at one of the guns & for this brave action they have made him a Lieutenant which he fully deserved.

Now for a brief description of what I've done. On Tuesday May 25th we left our bivouac for the Reserve Trenches, by Jove it was a journey. Our way was by the side of a quiet brook (in ordinary times), but owing to a very heavy rainfall this pretty little brook turned out to be a raging torrent through which we had to march for a mile, in some places it was waist deep. One part we came to cross on a very narrow strip of earth; here it was that J.C.M. must do something clever. I put my foot a shade to the right & went headlong into it & before I could pull myself out my rifle & spade were carried down by the strong current. Needless to say, I've not seen either since.

Whilst on the bank feeling my whereabouts, as it were, the boy next to me was shot in the arm, so after assisting to dress it I took his rifle & continued my weary way up the trench which was absolutely indescribable. Eventually I got to my part of the trench & in spite of the slutch† & water, had a good night's rest. Lt. Brown was next to me & shared his blanket with me, but I'm sorry to say that three days afterwards he was killed.

The entrenching tool

On Thursday 27th we left here at night for the 2nd line of trenches where we spent the night & the next day; by the way we were still up to the knees in mud & water. Now came the day which I shall never forget if I live to be a centenarian. At dusk we marched out in partners, one carrying a pick, the other a spade; each had his rifle, entrenching tool & 200 round of ammunition, & a sand bag half full. We doubled across the open to the first line of trenches. We now doubled in open formation (a long line of us) for over a hundred yards further on & had to dig ourselves in; however the moon was full & before we had dug a single spadeful the enemy discovered us & opened fire. It was most awful; we were lying flat on the ground with no cover except a bag half-full of sand which has been proved to be not bullet proof time & time again. The enemy kept up a fusillade of rifle fire & *machine guns* for at least the

†Slutch - very wet sticky mud.

best part of an hour. I can't describe my feelings as I lay there, especially when four men on either side of my partner (Brockbank) & myself were wounded, crying out for help & we could do nothing to relieve them except put field dressings on the wounds.

It was no good lying there idle, so we set to work with our entrenching tools to dig ourselves in. Until we were 3ft deep we had to work on our back, sides & tummy, then when we had enough cover we worked on our knees. All night long we worked & by dawn it was up to our shoulders, so we sat down, had some breakfast, then to work again. We were now able to use the pick & spade & in a very short time we were able to stand up it in, so we set about to join up to the next dug-out in which were Baty & Smith. I can tell you I never in my life dug harder. I used to think I had done well in Khartoum after I had dug a few feet on the Desert, but circumstances alter things somewhat. I'm such an adept with the pick & shovel now that when I come back we shall have no need for the Gardener.

We worked for two whole days connecting the various dug-outs thereby making a trench, & at night we had to keep a vigilant look-out, so after our two days were up & we were relieved we were all jolly thankful, & I've spent the greater part of my time since sleeping.

The General complimented the Battalion & said that it was the finest piece of work done since the landing, so the 7th have proved their worth. Of course like any Victory or advance in this Hellish War, one realises there is very little glory in Modern Warfare, especially when you see your comrades, boys with whom you have lived for 8 months, struck down by an enemy which you can't see. If wars have to be, I prefer the old time warfare where every man had a sporting chance & the best came out on top. I consider myself & the other boys who have come through unscathed jolly lucky.

I expect you will have heard about Harold Granger, poor chap, he was shot in the head & lingered for 24 hrs. He didn't suffer much as he was unconscious the whole time. If he had lived he would have been blind for life, so he is better where he is. You might tend my sympathy to Mrs G_, I'm exceedingly sorry for her & I know how cut up she will be. Tom Penry out of the 6th is killed & Capt. Smedley is slightly wounded in the leg; I'm awfully glad it isn't serious, he was so plucky during the whole advance.

I received quite a batch of letters from you today, also one from F. Butler. This morning J Richardson, Barratt, Thorpe & myself were practising hand grenade throwing under Lt Whitley, another new departure for me.

I haven't yet received the money. We have not much use here for it, although occasionally when we get down to the base we can buy a few things such as cigs from a man on the beach, so I think this will suffice me until I leave. You might send me cigs occasionally as they are awfully scarce, also a parcel now & then with some parkin & any other luxury (not too rich) & a tin of cocoa will be very acceptable.

Just got orders to pack up so I must close. We have now been in the trenches ten days so expect we are now moving to a rest camp. Kind regards to all, best love to yourselves.

Hoping this War will soon be over,

> I remain
> Your Son
> Jack

PS Send me a few envelopes. As you will notice I'm using old ones, the envelope in which I'm enclosing this one I received from the Georgiadi's two days ago. I'm absolutely in the pink of condition although I haven't had a wash or a shave for a whole week.

> The Mediterranean Expeditionary Force
> Monday June 7 1915

Dear Pat,

Just a few lines whilst I have the time. I wrote to Father & Mother a very long letter the other day, but I'm feeling a little bit dubious as to whether they received it, as being in the firing line at the time, I had to give it to one of the stretcher-bearers to take down to the base, & these poor chaps were awfully hard worked at the time that it's just possible that he may have overlooked it, & I can't think for the life of me to whom I gave it, however I hope they've got it.

We've just gone through it, but no doubt it will be in the papers before you get this. I must say that I feel awfully proud to be in in a unit in such a brigade but I would not like to go through it again for £1000.

The charge took place last Friday. At 10 o'clock a very heavy bombardment of the enemy's trenches by our artillery took place & at 12 o'clock we made the bayonet charge; having taken their first line of trenches our Company rushed on to what we took to be their second line, but on arriving there we found it to be only a sham one & more than half of us had to lie down in the open with no cover & the enemy were firing on us from the front & also the right flank. We then got the order to retire to the first trench we had taken, which was about 500 yards in the rear, so off we started at the double. It seemed to be an awfully long 500 yards, as after advancing about 1000yds we were pretty nearly jiggered. On I ran with the bullets whistling past & men on either side of me dropping down shot. I fell twice from sheer exhaustion & at last finished up walking. At last I reached the trench & dived over the parapet like a shot rabbit, none the worse thank God, but absolutely jiggered.

You will understand how lucky I am when I tell you that there are only four of we Stockport lads who are not wounded, namely Denby, Green, Sykes & myself, of course Sykes wasn't in it as he was a ration carrier. Baty slightly wounded in the shoulder, J Hulme slightly wounded, H.Smith wounded in legs, Barratt slightly wounded, F Lomas missing, J Richardson slightly wounded, J Holland missing, H Holland wounded seriously, Eddie Granger is missing up to writing, but don't say anything to Mrs G_ about it as it's just possible he may turn up. I hope so because as I told you in the last letter, Harold is killed & it would be terrible if Eddie doesn't get home again.

Billie Moss is also in hospital, he had a nervous breakdown after the first advance. I'm sorry to say that Major Staveacre is killed[†], without any doubt he was the finest Officer in the Battalion.

We are now in the support trenches, there are only 20 of us left in my Platoon which numbered 58 when we first arrived here, all the others are either dead or else on the hospital ship. My pal Brockbank is also wounded, but I envy him as it's only slightly in the hand & he'll be having quite a decent holiday on the hospital ship.

Before closing I'll just remind you in case you didn't receive my last letter, that a few cigs, some parkin or cake, a tin of cocoa and any other little tasty bit will be very acceptable, also enclose a few envelopes & an indelible pencil.

Wednesday June 16 1915
The Mediterranean Expeditionary Force

Dear Mother & Father,

I'm writing this on one of the small islands belonging to ( ). Now that we have done what was required of us & made a name for our Battalion we have come here for a rest. It's an ideal little spot & there is a very fine bathing beach where we have our daily dip. The boys of the Sixth are encamped next to us, but I'm sorry to say that they have been hit quite as hard as us. There are only four of the boys here namely Stanley Cragg, Edgar Lomas, Billy Bourne & Harold Lingard, the others are either in hospital, missing or killed, so when we meet it's a jolly sight less of a crowd than in Cairo.

There is nothing on the island except a few Greeks who have opened about six booths where we can buy chocolate and other tit-bits at extortionate prices, but after being five weeks without a chance of buying such delicacies we willingly pay it.

We get plenty of good food, every morning bacon for breakfast, so I take a trip up to the Greeks, buy a couple of eggs & fry them with my bacon. Usually on my buying-in trips

[†]4th June. He was writing a report in the trench when he was shot by a sniper.
Another version is that he was directing ammunition supplies.

71

before breakfast I meet Stanley Cragg doing the same. At present in my tent there is only Sykes whom you know, all the others are either in hospital or killed. I gave you details in my last letter so I won't agonise again.

There are tons of rumours floating around as to where we are bound for when we leave here, the most predominant one is that we are coming home, well I hope it is correct. We have just heard that Rumania, Bulgaria & Greece have joined the Allies cause. I'm off now to the ( ) lines so will close.

Tuesday June 29th 1915

I'm writing this in the firing line after having spent a very pleasant week strolling round a small Island† where we went for a rest. We are now back carrying on with the good work. According to rumour our Division will be home sometime in July, so I eagerly waiting for this month to close, then we shall see if *General Rumour* is correct this time.

I can't say how the other boys are, as after they are taken to hospital we very rarely hear anything of them until they come back to us, but I think you can take it from me that they are doing well because, true to the old saying that bad news travels quickly, we usually hear from some source or other if their condition is precarious.

In one of my previous letters I mentioned that Douglas Green was all right. Well, I'm sorry to say that the day after I wrote he went on an errand with another fellow and never returned, but I believe his body was found in a gully. I wouldn't write such depressing news only I know that you will hear from Mr & Mrs Green as I wrote so recently saying that he was alright. I thought it quite possible that when you told them they might hold on to a false hope that there was a mistake.

I am in the best of health and the only things which bother me are the flies. They are absolutely abominable, in fact they are a greater curse than the --------. I received your letter of the 4th from the Officer, also Mother's with no date on, but I received it at the same time. I'm looking forward to the parcel which you mention. I have also received this week 2 letters from Pat & the cigarettes which are a real treat after the awful stuff I've had to smoke out here.

On my way up to the trenches the other day, who do you think I met coming down, Bernard Horner, he has a Commission in the Fusiliers. It's awfully funny coming across boys like this, both of you having a full pack on & looking more like pack mules than peaceful Stockport citizens.

I might say before closing that during the week's rest I had some very novel excursions with

†Imbros

Joe Chatterton & Harold Breton visiting native villages & pinching pears etc which we stewed. Best love to you all, hoping that you are all well

I remain,
Your Son
Jack

July 9th 1915

Just a line to say that I'm in the best of health though driven mad with the flies. I'm now writing this in the firing line where we are for a few days. This is about our 16th day in the trenches after our rest, rather a long spell, but there are good rumours that when we come out we are being relieved, so keep smiling; although just outside my parapet there is a dead Turk & he doesn't half hum.

When the parcel arrived I was on a water guard for three days. There were four of us on our own in two dug-outs & we had some really good feeds. The cocoa was especially relished at night before we retired. I would not have minded being on that guard for the rest of the Campaign but all good things come to an end, so here I am, back again.

Pattie advised me in her last letter to keep my head low; it's pretty sound advice, and I had quite made up my mind to do it after my first trip in the trenches. There is very little danger being in the firing line with a good thick parapet & every few yards there is a periscope so that we have an excellent view of what is going on in front of us without exposing ourselves at all.

The other day I saw a Chronicle of about June 13th where it gave several photographs of our Officers & also a small account of the charge we made. I suppose it would give you a bit of a shock at the time.

I sincerely hope that Tom's operation will be successful. You will all be pretty busy cheering Pat up. I was surprised to hear of you coming across Corporal Smith, he is most amusing, isn't he? At Khartoum we used to have quite a picnic when he was in charge of us & I must say that we could have taught him a thing or two in the way of drill etc, but like most of his nationality he can tell the tale very well. If you happen to drop across him again, remember me to him.

I was awfully pleased on finding the socks as the ones I was wearing had no heels. You need not trouble to send any more though, as I much prefer cocoa. I expect you will receive this somewhere about Mother's Birthday[†]. I'm more than sorry that I shall not be at home on that day, but I wish you, Mother Dear, very many Happy Returns of the Day.

[†]22 July

July 13 1915

Dear Pat,

Just a few lines to wish you Very Many Happy Returns of your Birthday[†]. I don't know whether this will reach you in time, as from all accounts letters from here appear to take longer in delivery than from Khartoum. In Father's last letter he said that it was five weeks since you received my last one, well I can't understand it as I write each week.

Tell Mother that yesterday I received her second parcel, the parkin is absolutely superb & the handkerchief will seare (sic) any Turks I come across although they are pretty keen on bright colours.

You will be pleased to hear that Jack Richardson came back yesterday none the worse for his bullet wound in the foot. He has had quite a good time in Alexandria.

I sincerely hope that by the time you receive this Tom will have quite recovered from his operation. By the way, if I should not have the luck to come off this place alive, you can give Tom the pipe that Mr B_ sent to me. Of course I don't suppose you will have to give it to him, but I just mention it so that in any case the pipe will have a *good home*.

Tell B_ that I will write to her at the 1st opportunity. Yesterday we had a grand coup, capturing $\frac{1}{2}$ a dozen lines of trenches, hundreds of prisoners & 6 German Officers. I wish I had charge of the latter.

Yesterday I got hold of a Stockport Paper with Major Staveacre's & Harold Granger's photograph in. I must close now as I've just about time for a wash before moving into the line again. Remember me to Tom & family. Best love to yourself, Father & Mother.

I remain
Your Brother
Jack

Sunday July 18th 1915

Just a line to say that I'm in the pink, in fact this life seems to suit me. At present we are in a dug-out.

I think I have told you that the 2nd parcel has arrived & has been made very good use of, even to the wooden box which I prize nearly as much as the contents. Out here wood is more precious than gold. Many a time I should have had a cold meal if it had not been for the wooden box. The tin opener is also a very useful thing to have.

[†]24 July 1889.

I had quite a batch of news by the last post. I had letters from Tom, Patty, yours & Father's & two from Rivelyn†, & who do you think sent me two packets of cigarettes? Walter Ackroyd, awfully decent of him wasn't it? I will write to him when I have the time, but in the meantime you might thank him. I was awfully pleased to read in your letter that Marshall was recovering well.

I am not in need of any shirts etc. Pleased to hear that Tom's operation has been successful & hope that he will keep on doing well. Pleased to hear that you received my letters. I must close now as I've absolutely nothing more to say.

Sunday July 25th

My dear Mother,

I am so pleased to hear that you are keeping well, as I know what with worrying & hearing about what has happened here you are going through it much more than I am, but as you say in your letter Special Providence is watching over me, so you need not fear for my safety. You are doing a very wise thing going to Ansdell & if you will take my advice you will stay there a month or so as I'm sure a change of air & surroundings will do you good.

I have now received your third parcel containing parkin & chocolate & handkerchiefs. Give Mrs Ellis my best thanks for the Waverly chocolates, they were delicious. By the way, the contents are in much better condition when the tin box is enclosed in a wooden one.

I cannot say much more except that I'm back in the trenches & am still in the best of health. Kind regards *Mispah*

Sunday July 25 1915

My Dear Father,

This is in reply to yours of the 4th. You say that you have seen Forshaw & Woodworth. I think that the latter is Woodhouse is it not? Remember me to them next time you see them. I was surprised to hear that D Lister & H Smith were in England, the lucky dogs. I do envy them.

You say that you think we deserve a rest & so we do, but I'm afraid that we are a long way from having one. I'm sorry to say that nothing more has been heard of J Holland or Lomas. You ask me if I know anything of Barber of the 6th, well I don't & I can't give you any

†The Hardman's home in Bury.

more information now as I'm in the trenches, but as soon as I get the opportunity I'll go over & make enquiries.

I have received the cigarettes all right & Crossdale also enclosed a packet of his own brand with his compliments. The other day a box of 50 cigs came for Marshall from his Father. Nobody knew where he was, so the Quartermaster of the Company said it was the usual custom in cases like these for his comrades to have them, so I took them & divided them among the few Stockport lads who are left. You might tell Mrs Bateman.

Things have been awfully quiet here during the last week & I have no news whatever. I must not forget to say how delighted I was with your photograph. You have still got the stern old expression on your dial, you know the look, "Touch me not, I'm C.S.M.", and your Little Mary is as corpulent as ever. You say you are out for a few days motoring, but you don't say where. From the photo it looks a bit like the Dee.

You need not bother about sending me shirts etc as it's all the more weight to carry about with me. Of course with regard to socks, if Mother would enclose a pair, say, with every 3rd parcel I shall be nicely fixed up. Remember me to Bateman's etc. Best love to yourselves.

———————————————————

Sunday July 25th 1915

Dear Pat,

I'm still kicking & feeling in the pink. It's a true saying, Mugs for luck, isn't it? I have received your letters of the 1st & 4th, also the box of cigs from Tom. At the same time I also received a box of 100 packed by Crossdale of Manchester, but I've no idea who they are from, as the ones Father had sent from there I received a week ago. Perhaps you will know, if so tell me in your next letter.

I am so glad to hear that Tom is progressing so well & hope that you will have a good time at Ansdell. You might warn Mr Barlow that when I get home anybody who mentions digging to me will go through it.

In your letter you mention that Eddie is wounded & a prisoner. Do you know this for a fact? Because we've heard nothing at all about him & I hope it is so. Don't forget to tell me if it is official. You might tell Mother that I did not come across Paul whilst I was staying at Imbros.

Father asked me in his letter who was in command now. About a week ago our new Colonel joined us, Colonel Canning. Whilst we were at Cairo Captain Fawcus[†] joined us & came out here with us. Previous to joining us he had seen service in East Africa with the scrap there

---

[†]Captain Fawcus was the only combatant officer to land with them on the Peninsula and remain until the evacuation.

against the Germans. He was the man left to take command in our charge & I must say he was just the man for it.

Yesterday I saw Lieutenant Joe Kirk, he was awfully cut up about his brother Tom. I can't find any more news for you so will close. Thank Tom for the cigs & tell him that I will write to him at the first opportunity. Give Beatrice my love. Kind regards to all.

PS. Don't forget to let me know about Eddie Granger

Sunday August 1st 1915

My Dear Mother,

This is in reply to yours of July 8th. By the same mail I also received the papers from Father & four days ago I received the 4th parcel containing cocoa, tinned fruit, chocolate, lemon roll, screwdriver & patent cigarette lighter. By the way, was the licorice sent at Lena's instigation? It's like one of her practical jokes. I might mention that I have no use for it.

This life agrees with me tip-top. Since being on the Peninsular, yesterday I paid my first visit to the Doctor as I had a slight attack of diarrhoea. The cigarette lighter will be most useful as I'm one of the Battalion Bomb-throwers and it's the very thing for lighting them with. I've been puzzling my head what you've included a screwdriver for, but up to now I've not solved the problem.

I'm now digging out with Thorpe who had a parcel at the same time, so I'll just give you the menu of our dinner the day the parcels arrived: haricot soup made from Lazonby's soup tablets, bread pudding made from our rations of currants & raisins, stewed peaches with Nestle's milk (which were most luscious), lemon roll, not bad fare for the trenches & yet you hear people talk about the hardships of Active Service.

I'm awfully glad you wrote to Lt. Brown's people. Do you know, in our Company we have only one Officer left who was at Khartoum with us & he is Lt Whitely. All the others are fresh from England. Arthur Haydon is awfully lucky having two weeks furlough. Have you heard any more about Eddy? If you do, let me know at once. I might mention that Major Hertz rejoined us yesterday.

I hope that Tom will now have regained his health & spirits & that you are all feeling better at Ansdell. Just fancy, this time last year I was writing to you from Port Erin. I never in my wildest dreams thought I should come here for my August Bank Holidays. It's awfully invigorating what with the sea & sea shells & other shells etc. It absolutely takes one out of our ordinary routine. It's a fine place for anyone suffering from overwork; out here they will forget about business worries.

Thursday August 5th 1915

Just fancy, it is now August 5th & here I am still on the heels of the Terrible Turks.

By the last mail I received 100 cigs packed up by Crossdale & a letter from Mother dated July 13th in which she says that you have not received any letters from me for a long time. Well I can't understand it as I write at least once a week & always say whether I have received the parcels. In fact I have always acknowledged them as I have received them & up to writing I have received four & they've been jolly good.

Captain Smedley rejoined the Battalion yesterday, but sorry to say he is not now attached to our Company. I am delighted to hear that Eddy is being well treated in Constantinople. Father asked me if I had heard anything about J Holland & F Lomas. I don't know anything about J Holland but F Lomas got an awfully nasty bullet right through his head so that even if he was taken prisoner I am afraid he would not have much chance of living.

I will now have ten minutes interval to eat my pobs†; being rather fed up with Army food, Thorpe & myself have found a new diet of bread & milk made from Nestles condensed milk which we can now buy at 1/- a tin from the canteen which has been opened on the Beach.

I might say that the Stockport contingent is growing less, as since last I wrote you, Joe Chatterton, W Sykes & J Richardson have been sent to the sick hospital, and three days ago Harold Breton was slightly wounded; and through it all Jack is like Johnny Walker's Whisky, still going strong.

I'm writing this in my bomb-proof shelter in the firing line where we have been for four days, but are getting relieved tonight. By the way, whilst being out here, the other day an Officer who was reviewing the situation asked me if I knew Grangers & Baty. He heard that Harold had been killed, but he was awfully pleased when I told him that Eddy was safe, and that Baty was getting on all right. I don't know his name but he was with them at the St Anne's School.

Had some awfully good sport this morning, two of us together, one with the periscope the other with his rifle. Some of these Turks are awfully cheeky; they walk about the trenches with their head & shoulders showing above the parapet; the one with the periscope spotted them & told the other where to fire. Between us we bagged quite a few. In fact to put it in the sporting line of phrase, we got quite a good bag.

---

†Pobs - cubes of bread in hot milk.

Lt Whitely went down to hospital today, (nothing serious, just a bit run down) so now we have not got one Officer in the Company who was with us at Khartoum & the majority of the new Officers just come out are not a patch on the original ones. I have not any more news so will close. Kind regards to Smiths, Bournes, Brooks, Fletchers, Ellis, Aunt Alice & Family, also Hardmans, also remember me to *Mrs Harrison*. Best love to yourselves & Pat.

I remain
Your Son
Jack.

Sunday Aug 8th 1915

My dear Mother,

This is in reply to your letter of July 20th from Ansdell. I hope the sea air has had the desired effect and that you are all feeling better for the change.

You say that a fellow named Hulme called at the office when Father was out. It would be Jack Hulme with whom I worked at B & J's. He was wounded in the charge of June 4th, so after being at Malta he has come home.

No doubt you will read in the papers that the boys of the Manchester Brigade made another charge yesterday. Do not let it trouble you as I'm still in the pink, although I've had one or two narrow shaves, but up to writing no Turkish lead has found a home in me, thank God.

It is awfully strange that you do not seem to be getting all the letters I write, but after leaving me they go through so many hands that ten-to-one many of them get mislaid. Of course I've no doubt that you will now have received my acknowledgements of the parcels. Up to writing I've had four containing cake, parkin, tinned fruit etc.

The other day we had just returned from the firing line into some trenches behind & who do you think I met but Douglas Stephenson. He is a Captain in the 9th Manchesters. He came out about three weeks ago, so we had quite a good chat. It's awfully nice to come across somebody who has just come out from dear old Stockport.

I had a letter from Mr Granger this morning telling me that Eddy is wounded at Istanbul. I must say that all the boys in the Battalion along with myself are delighted to hear that he is safe & we are hoping that some of the others reported missing will be with him.

Sunday Aug 8th 1915

Dear Tom & Pat,

This is in reply to yours from Ansdell. I do enjoy your joint letters; I can't describe my feelings altogether, I always feel most cheerful after reading them, then I have a deep feeling of sympathy for both of you to think that you have still got it badly; to put it plainly, I can just picture your heads together at the table, scrapping every now & then as to which one should write this or that, and then after going through a great deal of chin-wagging, you would come to terms.

Well Tommy, after all this kid, I might as well tell you that I'm delighted to hear how well you are progressing & hope that you will keep on with the good work. Take things easy & don't let your little Queen drag you all over the place.

Now a word of advice to Pat: Tom tells me that at Ansdell there are plenty of old maids (2 for 1d) so you had better guard your invalid well. Don't give him too much spending money or he might be bringing a brace home some night. I hope this won't bore you but there is no news so I have to talk a lot of piffle to make up. At present I'm doing two things, writing this & making a rice pudding & every second I have to jump up to prevent it boiling over. It's a most ticklish job making a rice pudding.

I had quite a long chat with Douglas Stephenson yesterday. In your letter you say that Joynson Hicks was speaking in Parliament about us having a furlough. Well I hope his words have the needful effect.

You might give Arnold my heartiest congratulations, I was astounded on hearing about Sam. I've just heard that Stan Cragg was slightly wounded in yesterday's charge.

I might tell you I just missed having a nice wound myself. Last night I was stood up in the trench with my equipment on & a bullet just grazed my arm & buried itself in a case of cartridges which were in my pouch. Awfully lucky wasn't it? And it did not even draw blood as the mark on my arm is just as though I had scraped it on the sides of the trench. I hope to God that I shall be back among you before long & if the summer is not quite over, have a short time at Port Erin. Kind regards to Tom's people.

PS. Best love to B_

_____

Lance Corporal Morten
August 16 1915

My dear Mother & Father,

Now I have a little time to myself I will make the best possible use of it, so here goes. I have now got a stripe, so in future my address will be Lance Corporal & not Private Morten.

For the past few days I have been Acting Section Commander. There were fifteen in my Section & it was my duty to dish out their rations & detail them off for various guards, fatigues etc. The one thing that got me down was every morning I had to go round my Section to see that every man was up. I expect you will wonder who wakened me up, I managed it somehow. Of course when you have been in the Army twelve months it's really surprising what you can do. However now the original Section Commander is back again he has relieved me of the job, so I manage to have a few more seconds repose in the morning.

One of the advantages of having a stripe is that instead of doing so much manual labour I'm more like a foreman (bow wow).

Barratt has come back, so at present he & I are living together. The last trip up in the trenches lasted three weeks & we have now come to the dug-outs for a rest. I'm hoping to God that we shall not go back. I expect that you will read in the papers that our Brigade has made another charge†. From the Military point of view it was very successful, but very costly in lads. The 6th fairly caught it, even worse than us. Stanley Cragg wounded, Billy Yates missing. Then no doubt you know, Billy Bourne was slightly wounded about 2 weeks ago & is now at Alexandria‡.

The night before the charge 50 of our men had to go over the parapet to reinforce another Battalion who were in an isolated trench. We had not been in the open more than about 10 minutes when the Turks discovered we were there, & they didn't half let us have it. We were all lying flat & you could hear the bullets whizzing through the grass. Out of the 50 there were 20 casualties, so I consider that I've had another miraculous escape. Considering that the Brigade is now only about 700 instead of 4 thousand strong (& we have had two batches out from the 2nd Battalion) they may realise that we deserve a furlough. In any case I'm living in hope that I shall have my next Xmas dinner at Arnwood.

By the last mail I had a very nice letter from Lieut. Brown's Father. I had a long talk to Henshaw this morning, he only came back from Malta about a couple of days ago. Have you stopped sending the parcels now? I have not received one for about three weeks now & it seems more like three months.

Now we are in the dug-out Barratt & myself spend all our spare time cooking. We make

†They went over the top at 6.40 pm on August 6th and came home at 3.30 the following morning having suffered heavy losses.
‡"Some of the 7th Manchesters were lying wounded about 25 yards in front of the trench and they lay there all day in the hot sun, not daring to move until night when some of them might be able to crawl slowly and painfully back to our lines - misery." - Gallipoli, Robert Rhodes James - The fight for Sari Bair, August 6/7/8 - 1915. This was in Gully Ravine.

some very clever milk puddings from rice & Nestles Swiss milk. I can tell we are fattening ourselves up.

Of course there are any amount of digging parties but I don't get so many now as I did. Remember me to the usual. Best love to yourselves Pat, Tom & Lena.

> I remain
> Your Son
> Jack

> Saturday August 28th1915
> L/C Morten

Dear Pat,

This is in reply to yours of the 6th. I do really enjoy reading your letters as a little scandal goes down very well even in the trenches.

I'm awfully grateful to you & Tom for the cigs. By the way, thank Father for his; I omitted it in his letter. From the tone of your letter it seems to be quite the craze now, getting engaged. I hope by the time I arrive back there will be a fresh craze or I might take the infection. Just fancy Arnold & all the Yates. Who are the lucky girls? Are they local ones?

By this last mail I received a photo of Beatrice in her uniform. She looks absolutely ripping & so clean in her apron that I hardly dare touch it with my grimy paws. It was such a contrast to everything about me.

Give Janet & all at Bury my love & thank Alice for her letter. Well Pat, you will get all the good news from Mother's letter, so I will close.

> Friday August 29 1915

I have today received your letter of Aug 7th & 8th respectively, also one from Pat dated the 6th. In fact I feel quite elated with today's mail as apart from your three I also got letters from Alice, Beatrice & Kathleen Smith. I had not had any letters for two weeks before this & was feeling awfully dumpy, so today's little batch cheered me up wonderfully especially when I read that there was another parcel on the way.

Last week I received the cigs from Tom & Pat & also a tin of cigs from Dick. He said that he

Beatrice

had been trying to join the transport, but I was awfully surprised when I read in your letter that he had joined & was off to France.

We are in the trenches now. Just fancy, after our last do of three weeks in the trenches they took us down to dug-outs for a long rest (so they said). We were there for five days and each day there was a large digging fatigue required, – an ideal rest camp. Well, the fourth day a draft of 230 men joined the Battalion. By the way, this is the third lot we've had sent out, & the fifth day we were bunged up into the firing line again.

I'm now getting very dubious about these rumours of a furlough, in fact I've been too optimistic & had some rotten disappointment, so I'm now turning into a pessimist in the hope that I shall get some pleasant surprises which will balance the disappointments I've had, but in any case I should think that I can safely look forward to having my Xmas dinner with you all this year.

You say that it is strange that young Eaton has not written to Greens with regard to Douglas, well it isn't, because Eaton was wounded by shrapnel about a week before that charge of the 4th June, & since then he has been at Malta & is not back yet.

The day before yesterday I met Frank Haydon & Billy Bourne in the gully. They were on their way back after being wounded & looked in the pink. I was on my way back from the bomb school where I had spent a week. Of course you know I have been a bomb-thrower all along, but the week I spent at the school was chiefly tuition in the art of making them & how to use a rifle grenade etc.

I was surprised to hear that my name was spoken aloud at the Service held in St George's Church on Friday evening. I must say it is very kind of Mr Thorpe, but does he know that I'm not one of his flock?

I have still got a pal left in the Company as Hampson Barratt came back a week ago. I'm sorry to say that we are not in the same Section as we have now both got a stripe, so they have split us up into different Sections, but that is neither here nor there & it only means that we cannot dig-out together.

No doubt you will know that a few days after Richardson returned from being wounded he was sent back to the hospital as he wasn't well. I haven't heard from him since.

Now for the best news of all. This morning Major Hertz was walking down the trench when he called me to him & informed me that I was gazetted on March 11th as Second Lieutenant in this Battalion, but owing to some mistake the War Office have failed to make the Battalion cognisant of the fact, but he said that I should receive Second Lieutenant's pay from March 11th. So we are awaiting the official information from the War Office and my address for the present will be Lance Corporal, but I'm hoping that the next letter I write I shall be able to tell you to address me as Lieutenant. Not having been informed before has its advantages &

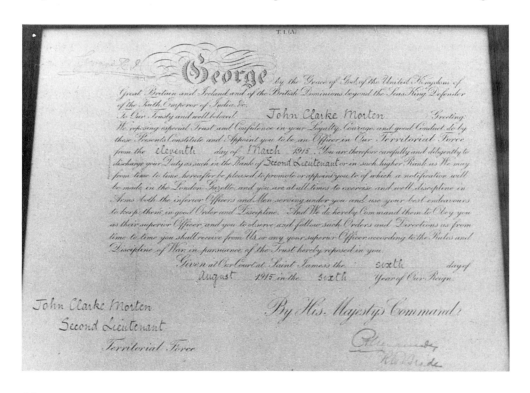

disadvantages. As a Private I've gained some very useful details in my experience although at times it's been real hard graft. Then I've had less responsibility & I shall appreciate my position all the more when I get it. By the way, from what Major Hertz said, I understand that the other boys who applied along with me at Khartoum have also got them.

It's awfully funny you coming across old George. He was in our Mess at Khartoum & we used to kid the life out of him. Remember me to him & I hope he will soon be better.

The 30/- which Father sent me I have acknowledged months ago. I received it just before going to Imbros. I must now close, hoping that you are all as well as I am, trusting to see you shortly.

2nd Lieutenant Morten
1st/7th Manchester Battalion
Thursday Sept 1st 1915

My dear Mother & Father,

I hope your eyes will not drop out when you see my new address, as it would be a shame if you were not able to read all my delightful news, but it's really true. Ask Father if he has ever been told the old saying that everything comes to those who wait.

It all happened in about half an hour. On the stage you see those wonderful transformations by the simple wave of a magic wand, like coming out of a hideous nightmare into a pleasant dream, the only difference being that it is real.

Yesterday I was called out of the firing line to appear before the Colonel whereupon he informed & congratulated me upon my good luck. Now came the problem of rigging me out, which was rather a difficult one as there are no Officer's kits in the Peninsular. Then of course whilst we are out here all that I require are decent clothes, whether Officer's or Private's, so I went down to the Stores & got a pair of riding breeches & an ordinary tunic. Of course I have got the stars on the shoulders as a distinguishing feature.

This being fixed up, I had to look out for a servant. Here again I dropped in very lucky by getting hold of a man who has about thirty years service in the Army, so he has plenty of experience. He came out with the last batch. He was one of the cooks in the second 7th and I might say that he has already proved to me his excellent capabilities at cooking.

Now I began to wonder to which company I should be attached, fortune favoured me again & I'm attached to A Company & the way in which he received me I think he was as pleased as I was. I have got charge of a Platoon & undertook my duties this morning. From the paper I'm enclosing you will see that I was gazetted on March 11th & of course my pay will rank as Second Lieutenant from that date. Rather sudden from 1/- to 7/6 per day is it not? Making a rough calculation I find out that the Army owes me somewhere about £80 apart from any kit allowance†.

Now look here Father, what I am now about to say, I hope you will see it in the same spirit in which it is written. When I joined the Army you promised me half my wages whilst I was in. Knowing how rotten trade must be with you, worse luck (for I know you would be happier up to your eyes in booking orders) now I am drawing Officer's pay and not Private's, it would be selfish of me to expect you to continue with the half wage promised. So I leave it absolutely open to your better judgment. I might also say that I shall not require any more money sending out, as I can draw up to £15 a month from the Field Cashiers, but as there are such few facilities for spending money I don't suppose I shall draw 15/- a month.

You might ask Mother to keep on with the parcels as there are four Officers including Captain Smedley in the company & we all wack in eachother's parcels.

There is only one thing now that would make me feel happier & that is if I were at home with you. Still the day will come. From mere existing I have now started to live. Of course, bear in mind it has done me no harm working as a Private on Active Service. I shall have a better idea of when a man is fagged than I should have had, but it used to get me down after being on some fatigues, coming back & having to cook my own food then wash up & have a fifteen minutes walk for the water. I am ashamed to own it, but today is the first day for three months I have had my meal out of a really clean canteen.

I must say Major Hertz was awfully decent & when the official news came he gave me a pair of his short trousers to wear in the heat of the day. As I said before I can get nothing here so I was very grateful.

You will see by the enclosed that all the boys who applied at Khartoum have been gazetted on the same date, so you might let the various people to whom it is of interest know in case the War Office fail to notify them. In the case of Wild it's all right & I expect Bert Smith will let Sutherland know.

You might let me have the following as soon as possible & take it off my banking account: wristwatch about 30/-, 1 pair braces, 1 ordinary leather belt for keeping my trousers up, half a dozen Gillette safety blades & two Officer's khaki woollen shirts, not too thick. I expect any of the first class Manchester outfitters will stock them, 1 briar pipe. Don't forget to inform Crossdale of my changed address.

I hear rumours of a mail coming in today so I expect the arrival of the parcel which Mother sent off on August 3rd.

---

†Presumably it was when his promotion to Lance Corporal was recorded in London that the previous Commission as Second Lieutenant was discovered. It was a long time to wait in ignorance!

There is a rumour that the Turks are going to attack us today, well if they do we shall give them a good reception & they will go back quicker than they came. So I must be off now to inspect my men's rifles. With very best love, full of hope of seeing you soon.

I remain
Your Son
Jack

PS. Love to Tom & Pat & all at Bury. You might send me the London Gazette every week, or whenever it is published. Friday Sept 2nd, the expected attack did not come off & this morning we have moved down to rest dug-outs for a week.

Lieutenant Morten
Sunday Sept 5 1915

Dear Mother,

Just a few lines to let you know that I received the parcel quite intact. Speaking on behalf of myself & the Officers of A Company the contents were A1. The lemon roll took the first place, you would be surprised in what a lovely condition it arrived here. One of our Officers from the South of England had never heard of parkin before, but he said he would try a piece. I might say since then he has had one or two more.

I am just recovering from a very nice light lunch consisting of dates & cream followed by pancakes. Do not think this is the Army ration, because we get just the same as the men, but Lt Woodward, the chap with whom I am digging-out, had a tin of thick cream sent out. The dates were an Army issue & the pancakes were made by my servant who is a splendid cook as I told you in my last letter.

At the present moment we are in dug-outs. Last night & the night before we had a concert. They were awfully enjoyable; for the time being they make one forget all about the horrors of War. These concerts are arranged by Major Hertz who is awfully energetic in finding amusements for the men. I don't mind how long we stay here as my dug-out is on the edge of a cliff. I have a delightful outlook; as I lie awake in the early morning I can hear the waves washing the cliffs many feet below & can see the island of Imbros across the water. On a clear day one could almost imagine they could swim there it's so very distinct. All good things come to an end, so I suppose when you receive this I shall be in the line again. Hoping that you are in the pink as I am, & trusting to see you again shortly.

Tuesday Sept 7th 1915

Your delightful letters of Aug 15th & 18th I received yesterday. I was awfully surprised on seeing how they were addressed, as I quite thought that my letters which I wrote about a week ago would be the first intimation you would receive of my promotion.

Now, Mother dear, you will be awfully disappointed to hear that I'm not coming home, but don't let it worry you, as I feel sure that Providence, which has so far kept me safe & sound, will watch over me & restore me to you in the sweet bye & bye. Then you must think of it in another way, Mother, think how proud you will feel when you see me leading my platoon up Market Street having completed our work here & to say that Achi Baba is taken & that we were in at it. Then of course, by that time I may have had another promotion. I might say that I was disappointed, but still, in these times disappointments will happen & they will make the meeting & the reunion far deeper & dearer when they do come about. So cheer up old dear, for my sake. As I told you in my last letter things are very different for me now. The few extra privileges & luxuries we get are an absolute Godsend to me, as I was getting awfully fed up with the drudgery of a Private's life, especially as all my pals had gone. Really, until one goes through it, one can't imagine what work an ordinary Tommy does on Active Service & I really feel proud that I was able to stick it.

Whilst out here I have been blessed with wonderfully good health or I could not have stuck it. I am still in my rest dug-out facing the sea & am feeling better for it. Then of course, any slight change of diet agrees with me. For dinner last night I had a tin of sardines & five pancakes (made by my servant). These little things go down awfully well after one has lived on skilly for five months. Of course this does not mean to say that you do not need to send any more parcels – carry on with the good work, especially the Bournville cocoa.

Well Mother, I'm sorry I have not been able to give you the good news you anticipated, but still the day will come & let us hope, shortly. Best love to Father & tell him to keep in with the fortnightly cigarettes.

Lieutenant Morten
Monday Sept 13 1915

Dear Pat,

Just a few lines to say that I'm in the pink & find the change still agreeing with me. We are in the firing line, having come up this morning after spending three days in the Duplicate firing line.

Perhaps it would interest you to know the routines we go through daily when in the line. At day-break which is about 4.30 am, the Company stand to, that means to say that all the men waken up & stand against the parapet with bayonets fixed. We also go through the same procedure at sunset which at this time of year is about 6.30 pm. I might mention that the duration of this stand-to is only for an hour & it is in case the enemy take it into their heads to attack, in which case they would find us waiting to welcome them, & much to their sorrow they have had one or two of our welcomes so I don't think they will bother us again. But in case they do feel like paying us a visit we are always ready.

I must give the Turks their due, they appear to be most devoted to their religion, & every daybreak or sunset they say or rather wail their prayers. Whether their belief is conscientious or whether it is a belief frightened into them by some priest or other I cannot say, however, in any case it is a jolly sight better than having no religion at all & I wouldn't object if they would do it quietly, but they have a kind of chant & our trenches are so near that every day at the stand-to we can hear them quite distinctly & it is most weird.

Of course I do not now Stand-to but I have to patrol up & down the line with the other three Officers to see that the men do not sit down. The Stand-to being over Captain Smedley sends word along for the three of us & we have a cup of tea or cocoa in his dug-out & half an hour's chat afterwards retiring to our dug-outs, usually for a little more sleep or if we are bursting with energy we read & write. Myself & the other 2nd Lieutenant usually go for the former recreation; I always have my best sleep from 6.30 to 8.30 or 9 am & as a rule don't waken up until my man puts the bacon & eggs (eggs are not an Army issue) under my nose, then my latent energy springs up & I do full justice to it. Breakfast over, I have a good swill, then at 10 o'clock or 10.30 am I inspect the rifles & gas helmets of my men.

I don't have much for lunch as it is so hot, but a favourite lunchtime dish of mine is to have one suet dumpling with Golden Syrup over it & 2 cups of tea (my man is a dab-hand at making dumplings). In the afternoon I do all my writing & have dinner about 6 pm which consists of steak & eggs or else a stew washed down with 2 cups of tea. My menu is not a very varied one but I always enjoy my meal. Then of course at times we can procure tinned fish & fruit from the canteen, but the demand is so great that usually by the time my man gets down from the trenches they have nothing left but eggs & milk. Then after dinner comes the evening Stand-to after which I get down for a night's sleep except for any patrol, which is for two hours a night. The four of us take different watches in turn. I prefer the first watch from 8 till 10 so that I know when I have finished for the night.

Now for a bit of gossip; yesterday I went out to afternoon tea. Our 1st Lieutenant is a Barrister from the South of England, awfully *blazy (sic),* a sort of second Rideal. He has a wife to whom he is most devoted & from the parcels he gets from her I should say it is mutual. Yesterday, there being a parcel mail in, he received five from her (I might here mention that I drew a blank) so he invited the Battalion Medical Officer & myself to have afternoon tea with him in his dug-out. We started with potted meat, bread & butter & strawberry jam followed by Petit Beurre & some awfully nice coconut & chocolate biscuits. It was awfully nice & might have been one of your "At Home's" the only difference being that I had to take my own crockery (tins) & servant to help him to prepare the tea. Of course the fair sex were conspicuous by their absence. I hope I'm not boring you with all this, but it proves to you that although we are all fed up we do our best to imitate & enjoy the things that can be had in the Old Country. I must now conclude. Best Love to Father, Mother & Tom, also Lena & B_.

Your Brother
Jack

PS Can you buy the air-tight tins of butter in Stockport?

Lieutenant Morten
Wednesday Sept 15 1915

Dear Father,

I have received your letters of Aug 14 & 22 & Mother's of 23rd with your little message written at the end. I'm still in the the pink of condition not even having diarrhoea which is most prevalent here, especially with the men who came out here with the last batch.

In your letters you say that I'm most fortunate in coming through safely the day of Aug 7th & 8th. Well I must admit that I'm very fortunate as it was a little bit hot, but I think the newspapers paint these little outings rather too gaudily so that the papers will appeal to the crowd. Don't take too much notice of the papers because as a rule, I think I give you a fairly descriptive piece of the actual engagements.

Last night I had a bit of a *do* of my own. After dark I went over to the parapet to scout out the ground between our firing line and the Turks, to discover if possible if they had any movement on foot. Their trench is about 200 yds away from the line that we are at the present time holding, & the ground between is rising ground very thickly covered with gorse, so that our observers in the trench cannot see much more than five yards or so at night.

After we had got about 20 yards from our trench we came across a gully. On entering this there was a bit of a scuffle, so we both lay down flat on our tummies & gripped our revolvers (which I had borrowed from my fellow 2nd Lieutenant). After staying for ten minutes or so, no other movements on foot, we crawled back to the trench (evidently Mr Turk thought he had better clear out, much to my joy). We then went out again about 200 yard further up the trench, & where we lay down to listen, & discovered nothing except that they were digging in front of their line.

In the morning, when I reported to the Colonel, he was quite satisfied with my discoveries, namely the gully in front, & that the Turks are in the habit of sending out a Patrol.

I cannot say that I am keen on these occasions, but when they have to be done, which is not often, the 2nd Lieutenants take it in turn, so that I have satisfaction of knowing that my turn is over. Little things & others here that we have gone through makes one think seriously at times & I am more pleased than ever, Dad, that you have always from my birth brought me up the way you have, namely to have a Christian belief, because I am jolly well certain that without it I could not go through the nerve-racking experiences that I invariably feel. No doubt you will feel that I am changing somewhat when you read this but I'm not; I'm still the same old two-penny worth (to use your expression) as when I left home. Only occasionally I have these serious thoughts and moods, a thing which rarely occurred at home much to your annoyance.

My new duties agree with me admirably and I have no trouble at all with my men. When I give an order it is always carried out with the promptitude and accuracy that you find in any Regular Regiment, and that is a great help because if there is one thing I don't like it is to grouse & grumble.

I am sorry I can't give you any rumours or official news of a furlough as the wild rumours we used to get have been very scarce lately. Perhaps it is as well, although a good rumour cheers one up for the time being, but I am still of the opinion (my own of course) that we shall most likely be at home for the winter, and I am not a bit downhearted in spite of one or two pessimists around me.

In your letters you never mention how Turtle House is doing & I should very much like to know, so when you have the spare time, just settle down to your desk for an hour or so and give me full details of what is going on. I won't order you to do it or you might get the hump, but I simply make a request. Of course nowadays it is second nature to me to give orders, so when I arrive home you will have a lovely time.

I wrote to Mr Fletcher yesterday in reply to his letter of congratulations which he wrote from Prestatyn.

I must now conclude as the smell of the steak & onions which is beside me awaiting to be devoured will not allow one to continue.

P.S. A parcel arrived last night, the Waverley Chocolates were luxurious, the pears Woodward and the other Lieutenant and myself had for lunch, the only thing we could enjoy in the midday heat. I can't express adequately as to how we enjoyed them. The parkin & especially the cake were put down as A1 in the Officers' Mess of A Company. We call it the Officers Mess – every morning the four of us meet in Captain Smedley's dug-out at 8.30 & have a cup of tea with a biscuit or a piece of cake.

Monday Sept 20 1915

My Dear Mother,

By the last mail which arrived the day before yesterday I received 4 letters, one from yourself & also father's dated Sept 1st and a letter of congratulation from Mr Brown of *Belfast*. I suppose he saw it in the Times newspaper.

We are now having our three week's trip in the Trenches; so many days in the firing line, so many in the duplicate trenches, so many in the supports and so many days in the reserves. We came out of the firing line two days ago and are now in the reserve, which is an awfully cosy little valley amongst the hills.

Owing to two very unfortunate incidents† which happened whilst we were in the line this time, which fortunately did not do me any bodily harm, I never felt so pleased before to turn my back on the trench for a few days. We go back again tomorrow for another two nights then we come out for our week's rest, which will be more than acceptable.

I don't think the troops in France do three weeks in & one out, do they? From all accounts it's just the Reserve.

Three days ago Captain Smedley was wounded again‡, not seriously, but he has gone away, so now there are only two of us in the company & I am second in command of the Company.

I have had some rather huge jumps in the space of a month, have I not? Perhaps you will think that I am wrong in my reckoning when I make out that one from our four leaves two, but I forgot to mention that our First Lieutenant had been transferred to another company who were short. You say they are short of officers at Southport. Well it will give you a good idea of how short we are when I tell you that at the present time no company has more than two, & besides myself there is only one company Officer with us now who was at Khartoum.

I went to see Douglas Stephenson yesterday. He was awfully pleased to hear the good news. You say Alf Caldwell is coming out here, well I'm sorry to say I don't think I shall see him as his Battalion is about ten miles from where we are.

You might thank Mrs F Brooks for the cigarette lighter. It has been most useful for lighting

†A mine explosion. Then a trench mortar shell was blown back into their own trench.
‡In the trench mortar incident.

cigarettes & bombs. I was surprised to hear that Stanley Cragg was on his way home. Harold Breton is also on his homeward voyage, lucky dogs aren't they? How is Marshall going on? I've not written to him as I'm jolly well certain that now he is convalescent he has more time for writing than I have, he knows only too well where I am & my address.

In closing I might say that some of Pat's lemon cheese in the next parcel would have a very cheering effect on me. By the way, Mother, have you got a photo you could send. I have one of Pat & Father & Lena but I have not seen your dear old face for over 12 months, so try & find me one.

I remain
Your Son
Jack.

Wednesday Sept 29 1915

Dear Pat,

Just a few lines to let you know that I'm still in the pink of condition & kicking. At present we are in the rest dug-out & enjoying life.

I've discovered some more pals on this Peninsular. The other day a Mr Smith called to see me from the 8th Manchesters. At the time I was having an early morning canter on a very nice horse which I have at my disposal when I have the time & fancy a trot. In the afternoon I called round at the 8th lines & who do you think Mr Smith turned out to be? I discovered it was James Balfour Smith (Katie's pal). He got a Commission in the 2nd/8th Manchesters & came out here with the last batch. They only arrived about the middle of last month & he is already sick & fed up with the life, so to cheer him up I related a few of my experiences which I have gone through during my sojourn here on the Peninsular. I fairly made his hair stand up & he could not make out how I had managed to escape both the Turkish lead or a bad attack of dysentery, as out here both these ailments are most prevalent.

As you know he is an absolute pie, but I was so glad to see anybody who had recently left Davenport that I spent quite a pleasant two hours with him.

Yesterday I came across another pal. Do you remember Nick Clarke at the Woodsmoor Cafe Chantent (Leo's pal)? Well I dropped across Nick. He is a Sergeant Major in the R.A.M.C. & he has got one of the best jobs on the Peninsular. He is stationed in one spot for about three months so he can make his dug-out practically a home-from-home, not like us – always on the move. He also feeds like a fighting cock, has a horse to carry him about & although he has been here all the time we have, he's never yet been within a mile of the firing line.

He isn't more than 40 yards from my present dug-out so I very often slip into his tent to have a chat & get out of the blazing sun. At the present time he is rather off-colour having contracted the general complaint which I have previously mentioned by name. Every day after sick parade an alarming number are sent away, so if we are here another two months there will be no Battalion left.

I called round at the Bomb School two days ago to see Lindley Henshaw who had a permanent job there, but on arriving I was informed that he had gone off the Peninsular two weeks ago with the usual complaint, so I went a little further on to see Billy Bourne & was told that poor Billy had gone off with a double fracture of the thigh & a few other minor injuries (2nd time he's been wounded) which he received owing to the Turks undermining the part of the trench where he was & blowing it up.

The same night I was pulled out of bed (at 10 o'clock). At the time we were in rest bivouacs & I had to take charge of 50 men who were going to clear up the wreckage & dig out any who were buried. I won't go into further details because to say the least of it, the things I saw were not pleasant. I got my men to work & by daybreak the next morning we had repaired the trench & made things something like what they used to be. This night nobody knew who was or who was not wounded, so I did not know about Billy until two days ago, & likely he will be home before you get this letter.

I started this letter two days ago, but I was so busy whilst in bivouac that I had to put letter writing aside for the time being. It is now Oct 1st & by Jove this morning & last night real Autumn weather prevailed, a very thick mist like one of Manchester's best fogs enveloped us & there was an awfully heavy dew at night.

This morning we moved up into the firing line for another spell of two weeks & I am now writing this within 60 yards of Johnny Turk who is paying great attention to my part of the parapet; in fact several times he has covered this letter with loose dirt when his bullet has hit the top of the sand-bag. It is rather wasted energy on is part because as long as Jack has got his periscope he makes full use of it & does not risk even a hair of his precious knut unnecessarily.

I saw Nip Heydon the other day. He is now about the only Lacrosse representative in the sixth. I have received Mother's letter of Sept 5th in which she says that A. Caldwell is on his way out here. I'm awfully sorry I shall not be able to see him, as the Battalion to which I believe he belongs are over at Servla which is about 20 miles the other side of Achi Baba. I wish him jolly good luck because the fighting over there has been very fierce.

I'm awfully glad to hear that Stan Cragg has landed in Scotland, & tell Mrs Richardson not to worry about Jack as he is better off where he is, even with an attack of fever. Mother asks me if I know anything of Billy Yates, well it is my belief that he is killed, as in that last affair in

August anybody who saw it or took part in it could not possibly hope to see any of the missing again. Of course I know that you will not mention the matter so bluntly to Mrs Yates, only I'm not going to raise false hopes in such things. As you know I always hang on to a straw, but when even that is not there to hang on to, I tell you in plain language my opinion.

I have also received your letter of Sept 3rd. Give my kind regards to Wilfred Yates & tell him to keep his pecker up. Offer my congratulations to Billy Sidebotham & my sympathy to Sam Howarth. If he can't sit down I think he would be upset with Active Service conditions where you have nothing but the ground to sit or lie on. I hear that Joe Chatterton & Edgar Lomas are still in Cairo & Harold Breton is on his homeward voyage.

Now, look here, do not rely on any rumours you hear about us coming home, because when we do leave this place I will cable the good news to you, so do not let any more rumours stop the good work of sending parcels, as although I am an Officer, the only luxuries one gets are from a miserable canteen which nine times out of ten is sold out, & even when we get them we are fairly rooked. The other day I sent my man down with ten shillings and in return for that I got one small tin of lobster, 1 tin of French jam, 1 dozen eggs & a few grapes. Of course when it's the only place one does not object to the prices so much, but the fact that every time you send down you draw a blank is very annoying, so keep on with the parcels.

In closing I must say I'm in the pink, in fact I'm disgustingly well. I sincerely hope that yourself & all at home, also dear Tom, are not troubling yourselves about me as I'm quite capable of looking after myself. Best love to Mother Father & relations at Bury & B_.

I remain
Your sincere Brother
John

PS. In your next parcel enclose a writing pad this size, as they are more convenient for carrying about than the larger ones.

Wednesday October 6th 1915
The Supports

My dear Mother,

Having received quite a decent mail I must not lose any time in writing or I shall get behind with my correspondence, but at the present time I'm reading an awfully interesting book, one of H. de Vere Stackpoole & as you know I'm not a great reader, but when I do get interested in a book I require some dragging away from it. Well, by a very supreme effort & giving myself a good telling off I have managed to tear myself away from it so here goes.

Yesterday I received your letter of Sept 12th, Father's of Sept 10th, Pat's of Sept 10th, Tom's of Sept 13th & a letter from Marshall who is still at Malta.

You will see by the heading that we are still in the trenches, at present in the supports having quite a cosy time except for an occasional shell or bomb which reminds us that we are at War with somebody. I've managed to get hold of some good novels & find it a most pleasant way of passing the time away when in the firing line. The last spell of three days I had there I read the Grey Lady by Henry Seton Merriman, most likely Father will know the author. He writes some very good stuff.

At the present moment I feel tip-top having just finished my midday lunch which consisted of four delightful pancakes, tinned strawberries with Nestles milk, followed by a cup of tea & biscuits (I got the strawberries from the canteen by a lucky chance).

Just had a visitor, our Machine Gun Officer, who sat down on my basket of eggs which I had put in a shady corner away from the blazing sun. Luckily only one was broken much to my relief, but mishaps like that upset one's balance for the moment until one has ascertained the extent of the damage, so you will see that bullets & bombs are by no means the most trying things you have to put up with on Active Service.

Yesterday some of the sick came back & I was greatly surprised to find a chap from Wilmslow (a pal of Dick's) in my platoon. He has not seen much here as he only came out with the last batch which arrived here in the middle of August. A few days after he went away with dysentery.

These last few days we have had some awfully good news from France. I think we have now got the Germans on the hop.

I'm awfully pleased to inform you that Hampson Barratt is now a Lieutenant.

Father mentions Denby in his letter, well Denby is not wounded but went off sick about three weeks ago & I expect by now the lucky dog is kicking his heels in Alexandria or some other civilised place.

Tell Father to keep the Chambers Journals until I come home, as I have had all along a presentiment that we shall be home for Xmas, although worse luck, I have no grounds for thinking so except my own convictions.

Patty informs me that the other night you went to the Palace. I hope you enjoyed it & if take my tip you will go pretty frequently. So long as they don't show any War pictures on the screen it will take you away from the Military atmosphere which apparently hangs over England at the present time.

By this mail I received another box of Gold Flake sent by Father & am now looking forward to the parcel you dispatched on Sept 2nd & others to follow in due sequence. Tell Father to thank Mr Plant for his congratulations. I expect by now you will have received my letters stating all particulars with regard to my Commission. I wrote it early in September & quite expected a reply by this mail, but no doubt there has been a delay with the mails so I shall most likely get it by the next.

I am still Second-in-Command of A Company. I have nothing more to tell you so I will put the lid on. Hoping that you will not let the disappointment of my not being sent to Southport interfere with your welfare in any way (I know it is a great disappointment to you & myself also) but keep your pecker up so that when I do come home you will look just as when I left, so that when I'm trotting you round to the Theatres & Music Hall I shall be able to do the heavy on the cash I shall have in hand, we shall be taken for brother & sister, whereas if you start worrying you will be old before your time. As you know my motto has always been ''don't worry over anything'' & 12 months of soldiering has not in the least altered my motto. In fact it has strengthened it because no matter how you worry, as long as you are convinced that you are doing the right thing (which I think I am by staying out here) things will turn out all right in the end. So the best thing we can do as regards coming home is to wait & see.

Give my kind regards to Lieutenant Thorpe, Best love to yourself, Father, Patty, Lena & Tom & all my other friends. Hoping to see you 'ere long.

I remain
Your Son
Jack

Saturday October 9th 1915

Dear Pat,

This is in reply to your amusing epistle of Sept 10th. I'm like Johnny Walker's Whisky ''still going strong''.

We came into the firing line again two days ago & expect to be in until Wednesday, rather a longer spell than usual, but owing to being short-handed, so to speak, it has got to be done. It is quite comfy – as you know there is only myself & another Officer in the Company. I look after one half & he the other & we get along quite merrily together. Of course our responsibilities are a great deal more than when Captain Smedley was in the Company, but having had so much experience in trench scrapping I think we are quite capable of holding our bit of line against anybody.

I don't know whether I told you but the name of my colleague is Woodward. He is a Kitchener Army man attached to us. This last week or so some fresh troops have arrived here, so we may possibly get a chance of having two whole weeks or so in the rest bivouacs when we go out for our well-earned rest. It is the usual custom when fresh troops arrive, for their Officers to spend a night or so with the Battalion who are in the part of the line which their Battalion intend to take over, so that the Old Hands can point out the various dangerous or other points in the line & instruct them generally in trench routine & discipline.

Yesterday the Adjutant brought to our Company two Officers from a Yorkshire Regiment & much to the amusement of Woodward & myself, this morning he brought us four Officers & eleven men for three or four days after which they take their departure out of the line, & I expect then for our remaining two days we shall have some of their Officers to instruct. It is most killing – I feel like a man from Cooks taking a tourist party round. You know the style although you may not think it, but the firing line, with its different spurs leading off, bomb pit & little weaknesses in various parts of the parapet which we know to a ''T'' (worse luck) take a great deal of one's time to explain thoroughly to a novice. Of course we had to learn so I don't mind passing the knowledge on, especially if it will in any way shorten our spell in the line. Then during our two hours patrol of the Sentries I have two of the Officers round with me so they will know the workings thoroughly & the two hours passes quite merrily with having someone to chin-wag with.

To put it in plain language last night was a hell of a night. Our land batteries, along with the naval guns were shelling the Turkish positions & lines the whole night. This was accompanied by the Heaven's Artillery, thunder & lightning storm on the sea & absolutely soaking rain. The position of our present line is right on the cliffs so you can imagine how the wind howled & blew along the trenches. The night was such a pitch dark one that we could not see the sides of the trench except when a red hot shell from the 12 inch guns rolled above us on its errand of destruction or a streak of lightning lit up the Peninsular as though someone had switched on the Electric light for a second. These illuminations were always preceded by the report of the shell when it left the Battleship in the first case, & in the second case the lightning was always followed by a huge roll of thunder.

At eleven o'clock my patrol was over so I wakened my relief, said good-night to my pupil & wrapped myself up well between two blankets & oil sheets & got down for the night. In spite of the elements & the noise of the artillery I was fast asleep in a very short time; but my slumber did not last more than a couple of hours when I was rudely awakened by one of the men who told me that Mr Woodward has gone toward the bomb pit & would I follow him. Well I opened my eyes & discovered that all the men in the trench were stood to arms, so I jumped up & went towards the pit, found old Woodward & asked what the trouble was. It appeared that about 1000 yards from our position the Turks had blown up a mine (which luckily did no damage except make a hole in the ground) but it was such a large explosion that our parapet & the earth in our trench shook as though there had been an earthquake, some of the chaps rolling off the ledges. It sounded so near that we at once thought they had been trying their dirty tricks on our bomb pit, but on arriving there, much to our relief, we found that it was not so. I told my men they could get down again & prepared my own bed a second time.

Just then Barratt & another Officer out of Three Company came to my dug-out to see what it was that had disturbed their night's repose. They were in the Support line & thought the same as we when the earth quaked. Well I put their minds at rest & got down again & slept until the Stand-to in the morning.

So you will see that I still retain my wonderful sleeping powers, even on hard ground & amidst shot & shell. A night like this is awfully breaking in for a new Officer as you will no doubt imagine. However all this excitement & discomfort was counterbalanced this morning on the arrival of Mother's parcel sent off on Sept 2nd. Also I struck oil at the Canteen today. I sent my man & he managed to procure two tins of *cream* for me, so for our midday lunch the two of us had peaches & cream followed by a jolly fine boiled jam roll which my man made. The afternoon passed very quietly, then for my 6 o'clock dinner I had a bit of beautiful roast meat followed by a piece of Miss Wood's cake & a cup of cocoa. I will now have to break off & finish tomorrow on account of the light.

Sunday Oct 10th

Now to proceed with my epistle. Being first on patrol last night I retired at 9 o'clock & slept soundly until 6 o'clock this morning which is the present time for Stand-to, so I got up & walked down the line whilst a cup of cocoa was being prepared. At this unearthly hour it is worth its weight in gold. I had a jolly good breakfast of bacon & eggs at 7.30, followed this up with a good wash & shave etc, so am now feeling quite a clean boy & at peace with everybody, & on looking very carefully in the mirror, I should think that my moustache has grown quite an eighth of an inch during the last month so that is very encouraging.

In your letter you say that Ester Gillespie has written to me, well I have not received it. Your news re Eleanor Robinson, Ellis Bailey & Minnie Aston very interesting also the *details* as regards your new costume. By the way, talking of Mrs Rowntree, where is Billy Staveacre now? I suppose in France.

In closing I must not forget to mention that the weather today is absolutely glorious, just like a spring day & the Turks are behaving themselves quite decently & except for the fact that we are in the trenches & hearing the odd bullet whistle overhead now & then, we would not realise we were fighting. I am still in disgustingly good health. I hope you are all well at home. Best love to Father & Mother, kind regards to all at Bury & anyone else who inquires about me.

Wednesday October 13 1915

I have just received your two letters of Sep 19 & 21st respectively. I am still in the firing line but having a very good time on the whole. The other day your welcome parcel arrived (I acknowledged it in Pat's letter) which cheered us up for a few days. Then when we had devoured the contents another surprise was in store for us – at last the Division have wakened up and opened a Divisional Canteen which opened last Saturday, so Woodward & myself thought of the early bird & the worm & sent a man off in the early hours of the morning to await the opening of it, & by Jove we have fed like fighting cocks ever since.

The various luxuries we received were Cambridge sausages, tinned fruit & cream, potted meat, pickles, Worcester Sauce, biscuits, Genoa cakes & last but not least a 1 lb tin of Irish butter (the first since leaving home) so you can imagine how we have lived since & you will not be surprised to hear that poor old Woodward has been troubled this last day or so with diarrhoea & tummy, but my old tummy is as good a pal to me as ever, so I think that the various mixtures which the Army has pushed down me for the last twelve months has made it absolutely proof against being upset with such delicacies.

Added to this we have the best firing-line dug-out I have yet seen & it is about 4 yards square, 4 yards high. It is cut in the back parapet & above our sleeping ledges our men have fixed up oil sheets which shelter us from the sun & rain. In fact I've seen many a small cottage up Oldham Road not half so cosy & homely as our little dug-out is. It will break my heart to leave it on Friday when we leave the line for our rest bivouac.

It is now Saturday. As you will notice by the date I started this letter three days ago, but in the meantime I have been so busy that I could not get on with it as we have been entertaining visitors for the past week in our dug-out. This last week some Brigades of the Kent Yeomanry (they have been turned into Infantry) landed here so we had several of their Officers attached to us in the firing-line so that we could coach them in the art of trench warfare, so when I was not inspecting rifles or other Company work I was busy answering the various questions with which they fairly bombarded us. They are an awfully knutty crowd. One morning, after taking several round the firing-line, I discovered that one was Lord Sacville, another was Sir Samuel Scott, then there was an Honourable Somebody-else. I believe that one of the Corporals is a peer's son. They are a fine lot in physique – I did not notice an Officer under six feet (rather a disadvantage in a shallow trench). Of course this work is very different from Yeomanry work, but they are awfully keen & I feel pretty certain that when the time comes they will come up to scratch. The Officers we had living with us were awfully ripping chaps & their company quite broke the monotony, especially as they had only left England three weeks ago. It was quite decent to hear them talk about the Old Country.

We are now in bivouacs again having come out of the line yesterday for two weeks rest, the greater part of which my time will be spent in letter writing. This morning one of our Officers went to Alexandria to get kit bags which we left there on our way here, so he is making several purchases for me in the way of warm clothing etc. This last morning or two have been awfully nippy so I'm preparing for what's to follow. He is endeavouring to get me the following: one Wolsey sleeping valise, one Burberry with a detachable skin or fur lining, one woollen cardigan waistcoat, so I think I should be warm enough *if* I have to winter here. Of course, bear in mind I am still of the opinion that I shall be home for Xmas, but in case we are not I shall be fully equipped for the cold weather, & even if we are I shall feel pretty cold in England I expect, having spent twelve months in the East. In order to meet this I made a special journey yesterday to the Field Cashier. I think I told you in a previous letter that a pal of mine has a horse which is at my disposal any time, so I sent round for it & therefore made my necessary journey into a pleasant canter.

Whilst I am writing this I am at the same time supervising the alterations which are being made to our bivouac dug-out as we have the same one every time we come down for our rest. So we are having very extensive alterations in order to be as comfortable as possible. We have not yet decided whether to have it papered or distempered, but I've no doubt the *Billy Booth* will offer his suggestions if we give him the contract. Putting all joking on one side, with the aid of sand-bags we are making it a home from home.

The has been a large parcel of letter mail today & we have fairly struck oil. Besides the parcel you sent me containing parkin, cake, cocoa, milk & chocolate & socks, we received six others. There are only two of us so most probably we shall both be on sick parade tomorrow. Four of them were sent to Mr Pain who was the 1st Lieutenant of A Company when I joined. As you know, shortly afterwards we went to another Company. However he went off the Peninsular sick a week ago & before going he bequeathed his parcels to Woodward & myself. So this afternoon, on the strength of all those parcels arriving we are having a tea party. The Adjutant (who is a ripping fellow; he used to be the Battalion

Sergeant Major but has been promoted out here) & the Medical Officer are coming round to our dug-out for afternoon tea, so I will report on the quality of the cake etc in my next letter when I have tasted it. Everything in the parcel was intact except the pineapple which, according to the paper inside, you enclosed. Well, there was no tin of pineapple in the box. Can you account for it?

Yesterday I received the watch & safety blades for which I thank you very much. I was especially pleased to find it was a luminous one; it is most useful at night when I am on patrol.

Captain Smedley is now in Alexandria. His wound is better but he is now bad with dysentery. You will be pleased to hear that Lieutenant Whitely is now back with us. I must now conclude as we are having our tea party at 4 o'clock and it is now 3.45. I will reply to Father's letter tomorrow. Hoping you are in good health as I am.

Wednesday Oct 20th 1915

Dear Father,

I have now been here for four days supposed rest, but I have had such a busy time that this is the first letter I've had the opportunity to write & this will be only a short one as I am quite behind with my correspondence & have about 12 which should have been written weeks ago.

In your letter of Sept 21st you mention about putting my money in the Corporation at 4%, well it is rather a sound idea, but what about the War Loan at 4.5%? Of course I simply mention this by the way, but have no doubt that you being in England and an *Old Hand* at this sort of a game, will be able to judge better than I which is the most sound, so I will leave it to your discretion, but do something with it.

What had the Draper's Record† to say about me? I hope you are well. I am still in disgustingly good health.

Post Card
Field Post Office
29 Oct 1915

My Dear Mother,

Just a line to let you know that I'm still going strong. I have not time to write a letter so you will have to be satisfied with a P.C. this mail.

†Private J.C. Morten, of the 1st/7th Manchester Territorials, has been gazetted as a second lieutenant. He went out to Egypt last September, and has been through the recent fighting in the Dardanelles. Lieutenant Morten is the only son of Mr C.S. Morten, of Picadilly, Manchester, who for 25 years has represented Messrs. J. Buckland & Co., underclothing manufacturers, London. (August 28 1915).

We have just received another draft from Stockport & although we have now been in bivouac for ten days we have not had time to write any letters apart from the one I sent you the other day. Young Eaton came back this morning after being away for over five months & I hear that Lindley Henshaw has also come back. I was glad to hear that Alan Preston was safe at home, remember me to him. Kind regards to the usual.

G.B. Hurst's book "With the Manchesters in the East" reports Morten left with a poisoned hand.

MALTA

Nov 8th 1915
Cottonera Hospital
Malta

Dear Pat,

I hope you will be able to decipher this. I can't use my right hand so am writing this with my left hand. Now look here, don't get excited & imagine that I've got a bullet hole as large as a football in my hand because I haven't. I scratched my hand about a month ago which turned septic. Our M.O. treated it but it got gradually worse & in the end cellulites set in, so they fired me off to hospital & here I am. It is most amusing – I have to be fed, washed & dressed like a baby. I am awfully fit in other ways, fed tip-top. Except for the slight inconvenience which I have to put up with on this account, but I am not at all sorry as at last I am having a rest, which I have not had for six months. There is only one thing I want now & that is to be sent home if only for a week. What a time it would be after my 15 months absence. Best love to Mother & Father, Tom & B_. Hoping you are all as well & fit as this letter leaves me.

PS. Is Baty still here? I've lost his address.

From Marshall Bateman

Dear John,

Take care old man when you go down to Valletta in future. Bear in mind you are not in Davenport. I am told you had quite a good time the other night when you met a friend ......
Should be pleased to see you tomorrow afternoon if possible. Say 3.30 at the Church (?)
Yours MB

Rec'd 6.50 pm 10 $^{11}/_{15}$

To Lieut. Morten
Cott H
Malta

Cable arrived awaiting your further news
Morten
handed in Manchester @ 9.45 am 10 $^{11}/_{15}$

Cottonera Hospital
Malta
Monday Nov 15 1915

Dear Mother,

Just a line to let you know that I'm in the pink of condition & my hand is now practically better. There is not much to write about only I must say that I'm enjoying the change very much. I meet Baty every day. We usually stroll along to the Club & have a game of billiards which is quite like old times. I have to be in at 7 o'clock so we usually part at 6.30 as our ways home are quite in opposite directions. I then take the Ferry across the harbour then a carrozin carriage & get back just in time for dinner at 6 o'clock after which I read for an hour or so, then retire for the night. Is Pat being married in December? If so you might let me know the date. Baty informed me that she was & I was awfully surprised as you had not said anything about it in your letters.

Union Club,
Malta
Wednesday Nov 17th 1915

Dear Father,

A few lines to let you know how Malta agrees with me. It is quite a different place to what I imagined, but I will not describe it now, I will reserve that until I see you, whenever the glorious day comes.

I am sorry to say that Baty has been sent back to the Peninsular. Last Sunday he told me that his name was down for going the following day, but neither of us thought he would as he had been booked for England for about two months, but on Monday he wasn't at the Club as usual so I rang up to see if he had really gone back, & they informed me that he had. I'm awfully sorry because I don't really think he is in a fit condition to go through the winter there, although he looks awfully fit. Of course, as you know, he always had that fresh look. Although I miss Baty very much I have still got one or two chums here who were in the hospital boat with me. Yesterday I had an awful surprise. I was walking down the main street and I bumped into Hampson Barratt. The shock was mutual as he had no idea that I had landed here, and when I left Cape Helles he was quite hale & hearty, but he informs me that shortly afterwards he was taken ill with jaundice, hence his arrival in Malta. I must now leave off in order to keep my appointment with him. Will continue later.

Having now left Barratt I will proceed with my letter.

I don't think I shall see the Peninsular this side of Xmas as the other day, when the Colonel was inspecting the patients, he came in to my ward. I told him how long I had been out so he said a rest would do me good. Of course by that he may possibly send me to Florence where there is a convalescent home & quite a number of Officers I know are going there, but I am hoping that my rest will take the form of a short furlough in England as it is such a time since I saw the old place. Of course you must not build up any hopes of such good fortune coming my way. If it does I will immediately wire you. In any case it will be a consolation to yourself & Mother to know that I shall be in a civilised place to enjoy the Xmas festivities this year. My hand is very much better & I feel tip-top notwithstanding my having lived in the ground for the past six months. I hope you are all well at home & not allowing the War to play on your nerves too much. Remember me to Mr Mercer, Mr Plant. Best love to all at Arnwood.

Sessions House
Lancaster Road
Preston
Dec 8th 1915

To Mr T.C.Morten
Armwood
Beech Road
Stockport

Sir,

War Office reports 2nd Lieutenant J.C.Morten, 7th Manchester Regt admitted 2nd Western General Hospital Manchester, November 29th 1915. sick.

H Hodgkinson
Colonel

From the Marriage Register of Mount Tabor Church, Stockport:
November 24th 1915†

Thomas Victor Hardman, age 28, of 12, Manchester Road, Bury and
Martha Annes Morten, age 26, of 29, Beech Road, Stockport.

----

†It looks as if he just missed this.

ENGLAND

No 5 Camp
Codford St Mary
Wiltshire
Thursday January 6th 1916

Dear Mother & Father,

Just a few lines to let you know that I'm having the time of my life wading through mud. You must not expect more letters now I'm in England because I've less time on my hands than I had on Gallipoli.

Harry, Harold & myself are attending every day a Junior Officer's Class & we are doing the

same things that we learned in Khartoum. We are going through the course as though we were raw recruits, we might never have been in the Army before. So long as we do not get too much of it, it will not do us any harm as there are little details in the drill which one is apt to forget when one has spent six months in the trenches where there is no such thing as drill.

Have just seen M Lees & he is quite happy & I'm glad to say there are some very decent fellows in his company.

Take particular notice of this, will you please go to Macbeth's & get them to send my new breeches & tunic per return, direct here, because if there happens to be a shower of rain when I'm out (which is very possible) I shall be absolutely in the cart as I have not got a change & would have to keep my wet ones on, so buck them up. You might also send my slippers per return.

Coming up here the train stopped at Stockport & Mr & Mrs & Beatrice Smith were on the platform & gave me a ripping cake which was devoured with much delight towards the journey's end. At Stockport Mr Fletcher was on the platform. Have no more time to write more so Au Revoir.

Codford

Dear Mother,

I wrote to you on Sunday & asked you to find a certain paper & send it on to me. It is a blue paper I think. I am having our badge (Fleur de Lys) specially made in the shape of a brooch in gold. I expect it will be ready today as I ordered it over a week ago. As soon as I get it I will send it on to you. Am off now to the class.

P.C. from Codford
Jan 11 1916

Dear Mother,

I received the mackintosh & the shoes this morning. The mackintosh does not fit, so what shall I do? Should I bring it over when I come or will McGruther want it returned at once. I have no idea when I am coming home but I think I shall at the end of the month.

Yours
Jack

Thursday January 12th 1916

Dear Mother & Father,

Just a few hurried lines. This morning we went on a route march (14 miles). Last night I moved into a fresh hut & today Harold & Harry have come in. There are just the three of us all together in a room which will not hold any more so we are well fixed up. What do you think of the Cape Helles? It was quite a pleasant surprise to me & I feel as though I would like to rejoin them. How are you both? I expect now you are so quiet all on your own I shall see quite a change when I come back. You will be a regular Darby & Joan for the present.

Codford
Jan 16 1916

Just a few lines from Codford.

I have no doubt that you will think that I am getting rather slack with regard to writing, but the week-ends are the only times I have for writing & today being Sunday I have written about 12 letters.

We are awfully cosy, Harold, Harry & myself in a hut & by the time we have completed the decorations we shall be O.K. At present the furniture consists of three very swell rugs which we got from Rylands†, a jolly good stove which gives out plenty of heat & yesterday we went on a buying expedition to Bath. We bought some green baize for a curtain to go in front of the door to keep out draughts. Then we procured some green casement cloth for window curtains, so you see we are going to be as comfortable as possible.

We had quite a good time in Bath & we are seriously considering spending next week-end there having quite decided not to spend any more week-ends in Codford than is necessary. It's an awful pity that Codford is so far away from home, because whilst we are attending the Officer's Class I have the week-ends free, only Stockport is rather too far away to come for a weekend. I have just finished afternoon tea & who do you think was having afternoon tea with the Colonel? Dr Schofield, so I had a few words with him and he has asked me to go & see him. He also told me that he had instructions to look after me.

Will you go through the correspondence I had from the War Office and you will find the various forms numbered. You might go thro' same & see if you can find the War Office form B.H. (it will have B.H. on top). It is a sick leave certificate & I cannot get my sick leave allowances until I forward this form on & I want to get the thing fixed up.

Jack Thorpe is a ripping chap & is looking after my interests. I'm sorry to say he is going

†Rylands - A Manchester store.

away tomorrow for one month's special course. I wrote to Mr Plant today. Have you had them round yet? I suppose not. I have not yet had the proofs from James, I wish he would buck up with them. I will now close, I'm fed up with writing, so Au Revoir.

York House Hotel
Bath
Saturday Jan 22 1916

No doubt you will be surprised when you read the address, but we decided to have a change of air this week-end, so here we are.

Tonight was the last performance of the pantomime so we went & met there quite a crowd of the Codford boys. We had an awfully jolly time finishing up with Auld Lang Syne & God Save the King; I have just returned to the hotel but before going to bed I have decided to drop you a line first.

At our little Hut we are now fairly fixed up and it looks very snug with the green curtains & the green baize door curtain.

One day last week I met Rowntree (Rene Staveacre's husband), he is in the Lancashire Fusiliers & I had tea with him in their Mess. This next week he is coming round to have either tea or dinner with me.

Bert Smith arrived here this week but I do not think he will last very long; in my opinion it is most ridiculous sending him down here; he can't bend one of his ankles at all, and it is quite bad enough for anybody who is steady on his pins, extricating oneself from the mud.

I don't think I have told you but I've had a lovely box of cigarettes from Beatrice for my birthday. The other day I had a letter from Mr Plant. In your letter you said that you would not ask them over until I came home, well I don't think you had better wait for me as our Division are awfully stingy with leave & I cannot see any chance of coming home for a while. It's an awful pity we are so far away because if we were nearer home I could slip home for the weekends. Harry & Harold send their kind regards. Hoping you are both in the best of health.

January 26th 1916

My dear Mother,

I do not know whether I have already acknowledged the receipt of the photos & the sick leave certificate. I have sent the photo to Innes today, the one you like, & have ordered 18 to be sent direct to Arnwood, but you must not give any away on their arrival until you hear from me, then when I know they have arrived I will let you know who to give them to.

The cake arrived on the day in great condition and it makes a very fine ornament to our Palace. I don't think the Codford air agrees with it as it seems to be wasting away day by day. The brooch I am sending off tomorrow certain. I hope you will like it; I have had it specially made in gold. The one Mrs G_ has is one of our own gilded I think, but there is no gilt about this one; it's little but good. I have no doubt you will receive the brooch before you get this letter as I sent it off yesterday.

I'm glad to hear that Pat's "At Home" was a success. Bert Smith & Malcolm Lees have just left my Hut, they have been here all the evening. Yesterday I had a card from Mr Plant wishing me Many Happy Returns.

By the way, for a Birthday Present from yourself & Father I would like a suitcase; it will come in very handy whilst I am down here for keeping various articles of clothing in & when the War is over for weekends, but I don't want a fibre one, it must be leather with my initials on. I think Tom has one, but still if he hasn't you know what I mean, a nice good *leather* one.

I started this letter four days ago. This week I've had a very exciting time; since my birthday I've not been out of my Hut. On Monday night I started with a cold & sore throat, so did not get up on Tuesday. The doctor came & saw me & has kept me penned up since. I am expecting him any minute now & quite think that he will give me permission to go out today. It's nothing serious, only one of my usual winter colds. Just fancy, it's eighteen months since I had a cold. I think I'll have to take up residence somewhere in the East after the War as the Eastern climate is certainly preferable to our changeable climate.

Don't be too critical on the writing, but the other day I bought a Stylo fountain pen & as you will see by the writing the flow of ink fluctuates somewhat. You might inform Father that I would be very pleased to hear how the new thing is working with himself & Mr Plant (Lyles). There is no more news so will ring off.

Codford
Thursday Feb 3rd 1916

Dear Mother & Father,

I have just returned from my medical board which took place down here instead of, as I'd hoped, Manchester. They have passed me for one month's home service, so I am stuck down here for another month. Our little trio has been broken up as Holland & Breton have made a sudden departure. They have gone to Hertford for a Junior Officer's Course. I now have our little Hut all on my own.

I have just received your letter of the 2nd in which you say that you have addressed a card to me for Bert Smith, well I have not yet got it. I'm very pleased to hear that the collars are a great success and hope that the repeats will flow in. In Father's letter he said that he had sent me G. Hick's address. I think he must be mistaken as I have not had it in any of his letters.

The Zepps have been causing more trouble & excitement haven't they? I'm glad they did not reach Manchester.

On my suitcase I simply want my initials putting.

I got my Burberry back from the Palatine today, they have made various alterations to my order and now it is quite the thing. I think I am going to Bristol for the weekend with a fellow who was in the 6th Manchesters in Gallipoli, afterwards coming home & getting a Commission in the 7th. My fountain pen having run dry I will finish up with an ordinary one. I was very pleased to receive the letters from Gallipoli which you sent on to me, one was from Woodward.

———————————————

Codford
Feb 6th 1916

Excuse me writing in pencil, but I have run out of ink. In my last letter I told you that I was going away for the weekend, however since then I have changed my mind, so here I am writing from Codford to the accompaniment of our band which is playing selections just outside my hut.

Yesterday, being Saturday, five of us motored to Bath. Arriving, we went to the theatre, had a good dinner, & at 12 o'clock midnight set off for our homeward journey back to Codford. It was quite a pleasant ride, the night air being brisk, and we were well wrapped up. We arrived at Codford about 2 am this morning, where each of us retired to our various huts to enjoy a good sleep.

Have you seen Bert Smith yet? He has come home again, not being fit for duty.

Tell Father to push the collars in Leeds & Bristol. If he should come to Bristol, tell him to come on a Friday, then after he has finished his work we can spend the weekend together.

By the way, when Innes sends the photographs, keep them at home & I will let you know who must have them, but don't send them down here. I will now close as I am writing under difficulty: in the first place I have no more news, and in the second place my dug-out is a sort of Open House, there is always somebody popping in. Whilst I have been writing this letter I have had about 1 doz visitors & to each one I have to say a few words before informing them that I am busy. Thank Lena for her Birthday card. Hoping you are both A1, as this letter leaves me in that condition

I remain
With best Love
Jack

PS. The other day I had a letter from Mr Brown, Belfast in which he asked me when writing home, to give you his & Mrs Brown's kind regards.

Sunday Feb 13 1916

My Dear Mother,

Thanks awfully for the suitcase. I like it immensely, it is just what I wanted & the right size.

I have spent this weekend in Codford & am feeling very bored. Holland & Breton have gone on a course at Hertford similar to the one I am attending here; I am seriously thinking of asking to be taken off this course because whilst I am on it I cannot get any long weekends to come home, whereas if I was with the Battalion I could, and I want to get home as much as possible whilst I am in England. Being a first line Officer I shall go out again as soon as the Medical Board passes me as fit; the Colonel has nothing to do with it. As soon as the War Office hear from the Medical board that a first line Officer is fit they write to his Battalion instructing them to send him out with the next batch. To tell you the truth if it was not for the anxiety which I know you & Father go through when I am out, I would go out with the next draft.

Father is always talking about me going in for promotion, well I have told him many a time that there is no possible chance of my promotion until I join my Regiment which is the *1/7* Manchesters. I am only attached to the *3/7* & therefore cannot get promotion here, and the longer I stay in Codford the longer I shall remain a 2nd Lieutenant.

I believe Lt Thorpe is coming back next Tuesday. Capt Smedley has not yet arrived. Do you remember me telling you about about a dug-out partner of mine in Gallipoli who lost his eye? Well he has now got a Commission & arrived here last week, so he is sharing the Hut with me. I will now close. Kind regards to all, best love to yourselves. Hoping you are well.

I remain
Your Son
Jack

The famous suitcase, weighing 15lbs empty!

Bourne Hall Hotel
Bournemouth
Saturday Feb 19 1916

My dear Mother,

After my arduous week's work at Codford I have come down here for the weekend. There are four of us, one being Harry Robinson. Have just come in from Boscombe where we have been to the Hippodrome. I am feeling somewhat of a knut at the present moment, sporting a new pair of brown boots, a pair of light puttees and a very knutty khaki collar (a stiff one). I bought them in Bournemouth this afternoon.

In your next letter enclose G Hick's address as I would very much like to see him, especially if he is going out soon. This place has altered, I would not have known it; the people here have got the Zeppelin scare and in consequence all the lights are off at night & the place is pitch dark. Then there are so many soldiers about that the place is quite lively. After dark nobody is allowed on the front; the promenade is patrolled & anybody walking along gets cleared off. For the present I have no more news so will go and have a game of billiards. Hoping that yourself & Father are quite well.

I remain
Your Son
Jack

PS Is Tim still going strong

PS You might please send me my soft cap, also please send my drill suit to the laundry, of course first of all take the stars off the tunic & don't lose them. You might also send me on the Tommy's tunic which is in my room (the one with the stars on). It is now Sunday evening & I have not yet posted yesterday's letter so I will enclose this note. I broke a record this morning. I got up early & went to Church (the first time I have been since coming to Codford).

Au Revoir
Jack

_____

3/7 Bn Manchester Regiment
Codford
No 5 Camp
Wilts
Thursday Feb 24 1916

Dear Mother,

I received your esteemed letter of 23 inst & note that you have done what I asked you, but you do not mention the soft cap. I think I asked you to send my soft cap but you do not mention whether you have sent it or not.

So pleased to hear that collars etc are going strong; has Father also got the Bristol ground? If not he ought to unless the naturalised *gentleman* has done him out of it.

I am awfully glad to hear that Marshall is coming home; I hope I shall be there to cheer him when he arrives. What kind of weather are you having? This week down here has been more like being at the North Pole instead of England. For two days the ground has been covered with at least 6in. of snow. It looks awfully pretty but I suppose we shall pay for it when the thaw sets in.

JCM and the soft cap

Last night I was out on Night Operations in a snowstorm. It wasn't so bad; just a little thin you know, but if only I had had my soft cap with me I should have been able to pull down the blinds & keep my ears covered, so apart from having cold ears I was quite happy.

This week several flittings have taken place. At the beginning of the week another 1st line Officer appeared (D. Norbury) so he came in here along with his cousin, which made four of us. Today he & his cousin have cleared out to another dug-out and another fellow has come in.

Last weekend was quite a pleasant change, the most exciting part of it was leaving there at 5.30 on the Monday morning, but we did it & had only one casualty & that was not very serious: only my poor old 1/- stick which I left in the train (this little incident took me back three years, on our departure from Tissington – do you remember?). No more news so will close.

Your Son
Jack

PS Thank you for the snapshots & G.Hick's address. My Photographs – do not give any away yet.

PS The soft cap arrived yesterday

Sunday March 5th 1916

My dear Mother & Father,

Just a few lines telling you the news. Last Friday I went before my medical board and they passed me fit for General Service.

I have received Father's of the 1st in which he informs me that he has paid the Palatine out of my interest. Has he invested my money yet? If so I would like to know where. Do not send my drill suit to me, if I do require it I will let you know. My influenza is now quite better.

Yesterday five of us motored to Bath. On arriving there I called on a Mr & Mrs G. Hicks & had quite a good chin-wag with them. They seemed awfully comfortable in their billet. I stayed with them until 9 o'clock when I left to meet the boys with whom I had come.

On our return journey we had some excitement: leaving Bath at 11 o'clock, we were just going through the outskirts of the city when we saw three motorists stranded. We pulled up to see what was the matter and saw their car in a field 10 ft below the road. It had taken a leap over the hedge, but marvellous to say, none of the occupants were hurt. Then we proceeded on our way. We had nearly arrived at Warminster (about $1/2$ way) when our tyre burst, so we had the pleasure of strolling about for half an hour while the man put on a spare wheel. We then continued our homeward journey and arrived without any more exciting experiences.

You say that you have booked for Easter at Craig-y-Don, well if I'm still here I don't think I shall go there as it would be all travelling, and I would much rather you had chosen some place which would be more easy to get at from Codford. I hope that you & Father are well.

Codford
March 7th 1916

I hope to have the pleasure of gazing on your dear old dials this weekend. I think it is about time I had a trip to Arnwood so I am coming this weekend. I shall arrive sometime on Thursday I think, but will wire you later if it is possible to come any earlier. Nothing more at present,

---

Codford
March 8 1916

My dear Mother,

Just a line to tell you that my leave for this weekend has been cancelled owing to some unforeseen incident. I am awfully disappointed, but still by this time I am pretty hardened to disappointment. I have no more news at the moment so will close.

I remain
Your Son
Jack

I am sending some collars home. Will you please send them to the laundry to be washed, then return them. They are stiff ones & therefore cannot get them done down here.

Codford
March 12 1916

Just a few lines whilst I have the time.

Yesterday being Saturday we had the usual motor trip to Bath. Arriving there the first performance was having a bath. We went to the Pump Room Hotel where they have a very fine warm swimming bath into which we plunged, afterwards drying ourselves with hot towels. Our next journey was to the Cafe for afternoon tea. At 7 o'clock we had dinner and afterwards we went to the music hall. At eleven o'clock our car met us & we started on our homeward journey & arrived at Camp about 1 o'clock. It was a glorious day for motoring provided you were well wrapped up. This morning I did not get up until 11 o'clock but have made up for my idleness by going a long walk over the Downs this afternoon. Norbury & myself had a fit of energy so we took the Battalion mascot with us. The mascot is a Bulldog, a most ferocious looking animal, but as quiet as a kitten when handled properly. Holland & Breton have now come back & we are all three together again in the Hut.

The photos Innes has sent are to my order: I only ordered one position, it is the full length one. I am awfully sorry, Mother dear to hear that you have been off colour & I sincerely hope that now you are quite better, & that you will keep in the pink so that when I come home you will still have your youthful appearance. I have nothing more for the present.

I have been contemplating transferring to the Royal Flying Corps. What do you think of it?

March 19 1916

I will now give you my usual weekly report although there is very little news. Yesterday we had our usual trip to Bath. I expect in about two weeks I shall have a weekend at Arnwood, in the meantime I shall be up to the eyes in work. The weather down here is awfully changeable, today it has not ceased raining, & such rain, it fairly comes down as though it meant it.

Yesterday we passed rather an interesting spectacle: there was a hunt & the hounds & the huntsmen passed right in front of us. Today I had a post-card from Marion (Dick's girl). They have left Wilmslow & taken a flat in London & I have an open invitation to go there for a weekend any time I like. It will be jolly decent as London is not so very far from here.

I have an idea that it is Lena's birthday in a few days, let me know the exact date. When you write you don't give me much local news; I wish you would.

Codford
March 29 1916

I arrived at Codford about 8 o'clock on Monday morning after having, changed four times on my journey. The draft that I thought I was taking out went on Sunday night, so it is just possible that I shall be treading the streets of Codford for some time yet.

I received a letter from you yesterday in which you state that you are sending my puttees on. I'm awfully glad you found them as I have had to wear my best ones, and by this time they are so covered with mud that one would never believe that a day or so ago they were a nice light colour.

I have not seen Capt. Jones as he left with the draft on Sunday night, but he bade me Good-bye in a letter which he left for me. Today has been ideal; it is the first time I have appreciated the country here & it looked really fine, quite different from the muddy Codford of a few days ago. No more for the present.

PS. You might send me my other *drill* tunic. The puttees have just arrived.

Sunday April 2nd 1916

How are you getting on? In your letter you say that it has been very quiet since I left.

Yesterday (Saturday) I went a cross-country run with the Battalion harriers. We did six miles & very enjoyable it was. Saying that since I came back to England I have done very little exercise I felt awfully fit after it. In fact I cleared off to Salisbury for the evening, but today I have been walking about like a lame duck, I've felt so awfully stiff in the limbs.

I went on Church Parade this morning & took the plate round. Next Sunday we are moving from here (the whole Division is moving) & going to a place called Whitley (I am not sure whether this is the right spelling) just outside London, so we look like having a busy time. Moving a Battalion is rather a big thing.

Tomorrow I am going on a three day's revolver course. I note your remarks re drill tunic & I am anxiously waiting for it, and especially the cakes.

Whitley Camp
Tuesday April 11th 1916

My dear Mother & Father,

Now I am settled down in my new camp I will drop you a line. It is a delightful place with pine woods abounding, and the Officer's quarters are quite palatial compared with the ones at Codford. Also the air is much fresher here & more invigorating.

There are four of us living together, namely Bill Lingard & two fellows who were out in the Peninsular: quite a nice quartet. We also have hot baths & water closets which are a great asset.

Last Sunday was our moving day & we came very well. Of course, being Sunday there was very little traffic on the railway so we did not get at all congested & having plenty of carriages we travelled quite comfortably. We are quite near to London, so I expect to be spending one or two weekends there. My address is

Whitley North Camp
F Block
Milford
Surrey

Monday April 17th 1916

I had not had time to write my usual Sunday epistle yesterday so here goes. In your letter you mentioned the mince pies. Well they arrived about three days before we left Codford & owing to the removing I forgot to mention them. To tell the truth I never tasted such mince

pies; of course no doubt I enjoyed them better then usual as I have had very few this year, but they were simply luscious.

On Saturday I paid a visit to Marion's at Sunbury on Thames. Of course Dick was there and when he saw me he was absolutely astounded as he had no idea I was in this part of the World. They have an awfully topping little bungalow quite near to where Dick's Camp is & he sleeps there every night, also has all his meals there; as I told him, he is soldiering under ideal conditions. We had quite a pleasant time, and the next time I go, I am staying for the weekend.

I am not quite sure how long I shall have next weekend, but if it is at all possible I shall join you at Llandudno. It is rather a coincidence, the man whom I saw in St George's School at Xmas is now my servant. Well I have no more news, so will close.

PS Any time you are cooking, a little slab of parkin or a cake will go down very well with our early morning cup of tea.

Monday April 19 1916

I suppose you will be home by Wednesday, so I am sending this to Arnwood. I hope you have had a good time & are feeling better for your holiday.

In my last letter I told you about my doings on Friday & Saturday, well yesterday I enjoyed as much as any day since arriving in England. It was just like one of the old Sundays before my life in the Army. In the morning I was on Church Parade, and at 11 o'clock eight of us motored to the West Surrey Golf Club and spent the day on the Links. At the start I felt somewhat awkward not having touched a golf club for so long, but I soon got into my stride & quite enjoyed it. The two golfers playing just behind me I discovered, were Mr McHenna & Mr Asquith's secretary, so you can see we were fairly amongst the B'hoys. Nothing more for the present so Au Revoir.

Saturday April 24th 1916

You do not know how disappointed I am at not being able to spend my Easter with you. Still, as the song says, ''Pack up your troubles in your old kit bag & smile'' so I'm making the best of it & having quite a good time on the whole.

On Good Friday Billy Lingard, G Norbury & myself went to Brighton in the Battalion car. The Colonel came along with us, but he was staying the night so we came back on our own. Of course, having arrived there he left us.

The three of us had an awfully ripping time. At 7.30 pm we went to the Metropole and had a ten course dinner which cost us ten bob, but now I come to look back on it I consider it was very well spent. Having finished dinner, feeling at peace with the whole World (except the Huns) we strolled down the Pier. Then at 10 o'clock we started on our homeward journey, arriving here at 1 am. The run from here to Brighton is a delightful one & the roads are in fine condition. It's a lovely car & we fairly ripped along. Coming back Billy & I had the back of the car to ourselves so we settled down & slept as though we were in our beds. Of course you know it's one of those long 20 horsepower cars so we were practically lying down.

This morning I went in for an Exam & answered every question. Of course whether they are right or not I cannot yet say, but I am feeling very hopeful & bucked up. It is now Saturday Evening & the three of us are off to Godalming or Guildford, so I will now close.

Royal Pier Hotel
Southsea
April 30 1916

My Dear Mother & Father,

I'm so pleased you had a good time at Llandudno, and it pleases me still better to hear that Father is busy.

Norbury & myself have come for a short weekend. It is quite a decent sort of place & very easy to get to from Whitley. Before leaving Whitley we caused quite a commotion: the taxi never turned up to take us to the station which is about three miles from the camp, & we only had twenty minutes to catch the train. Of course there are not many taxis in Whitley & there is a great demand for them, so the taxi people are very independent & it is quite a usual occurrence for them not to turn up. We sent three men to different places to get one for us. In about five minutes two taxis sailed up so we sent one back & were on our way to the station in the other one when we saw another one approaching us at a fair old lick. On passing I saw my Orderly in it smiling like a Cheshire Cat, but we had not the time to stop but left it for him to explain to the driver that he would not be required. It was awfully funny, though, having three taxis coming just because we happened to be going away for two days.

Have you seen Billy Lingard this last week? He is home on sick leave. Do you know, out of the four in my room, three of them have been away on sick leave; it's quite worth having a sore throat or mumps to get home for a week or two; so far I've had no luck in that direction. I have no more news for the present. Remember me to all.

Whitley Camp

Awfully sorry but I do not see how I can join you this weekend as the only holidays we get are Friday, then work on Saturday morning up until 12.30. If I came it would be all travelling; I should arrive Saturday night & have to leave on Sunday night. Hope you have a good time.

TELEGRAMS

St Budeaux Camp Plymouth
2 May 1916

Am going abroad. If you want to see me come immediately to St Budeaux Camp Plymouth.St Budeaux

3 May 1916

Tell Mother that I am here with Jack until Thursday morning

To Hardman, 12, Manchester Road, Bury

Thursday May 5th 1916

Dear Mother,

I am off in ten minutes. I received your letter this morning. I hope you will like the photo frame.

With love

Jack

May 12 1916

Sans origine

Arrived safely

17 May 1916

Alexandria

Landed safely

SINAI

May 17 1916

I am writing this from the Mess in the Best Camp, Alexandria, where we are staying for a few days prior to joining the Battalion. I think the whole Division will be moving in a few days but where to I cannot say, however as soon as I am in a position to let you know, I will.

We arrived here last Monday & as soon as I came into the Mess I saw several fellows I

Map of the Sinai Desert showing the Suez Canal and the route taken to El Arish

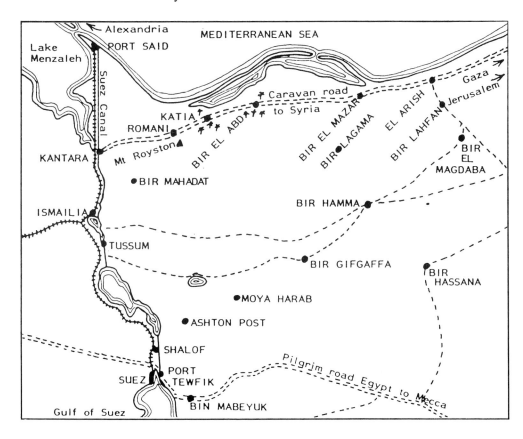

know. Capt. Smedley is here but I have not yet seen him. Vernon Firth is a Sergeant here, I dropped across him today, then a little farther on I met Harold Lingard who was just leaving the Camp in order to embark for England.

On our way out we stayed for a short time at Malta, so I spent five hours on shore. Talking about the voyage, it was most exciting, the whole way we had to always carry lifebelts & at night have them by your side whilst you slumbered. The whole day & night there was a submarine guard; I can tell you it is quite a nice pastime standing on the bridge from 2 o'clock in the morning until 6 o'clock a.m.

I hope you like the photo frame which Father brought back from Plymouth. I was rather fortunate, practically all the shops were closed & I had to purchase from which shops were open, & the frame I sent to you was the best they had or I would have sent a silver one. No more news this time, so Au Revoir.

I remain
Your Son
Jack

PS Hope you are both keeping your pecker up

May 20 1916
Alexandria

Dear Mother & Father,

No doubt you will be surprised to see that I am still in Alexandria. The Draft I brought out with me left here yesterday in order to join the Battalion who are on the Suez. This camp is the base for our Division & I am told that an Officer from each unit in the Division is supposed to be here, so I expect that is the reason of my not going along with the Draft as I am now the only Officer of the 7th here. I am having quite a good time as I have nothing to do, but I feel as though I would like to join my Regt & see Baty & a few of the old ones. I do not know how long I shall be here, neither do the C.O. or Adjutant of the Camp know. I may possibly join my unit when another Officer from England comes here, or I may not, because every Officer or man who comes out from home to join the Battalion comes here first, so whether they will send me along when the next Draft comes I cannot say. Providing I join my own Battalion eventually I do not really mind how long I am here as I have nothing to do except take an odd parade now & then.

My daily routine is:

Breakfast 8.30 am

Bathing in Stanley Bay where all the residents & other Officers bathe from 10.30 till 12.30 (of course mixed bathing)

Lunch 1 o'clock

In the afternoon I have a little snooze & at 4 o'clock I have afternoon tea at the Cafe in Alexandria.

At 7 o'clock pm we dine, & somewhere about midnight I retire to bed, so taking things on the whole I'm having a very lazy time. I will now close, hoping to hear from you soon.

Monday May 29 1916

I am still at Alexandria, but my lazy life here will soon be at an end as I have been warned to hold myself in readiness to join my Unit at any time now. Today another Draft has just arrived from England so I expect I shall take it on in a few days time.

Last Saturday I attended the Race Meeting & had quite a successful day financially. Today we have had a real taste of the Eastern climate; it has been most depressingly hot, not so much on account of the sun's rays, but one of those beastly hot winds that invade this part of the World periodically. I shall not be sorry to go as this life of inactivity & ease gets rather boring. Of course I have no doubt I shall wish myself back again in a few weeks time after having been scorched on the Desert.

Since leaving England I have had three more inoculations against "Paratyphoid" & "Cholera" so I think I ought to be pretty well proof by now against any disease under the sun. Rather strange to say the last time I came out I didn't even have a single bite from mosquitoes etc, but this time they have found me most appetising & at the present time I am absolutely covered in lumps where they have bitten me on my hands & arms, although I took the precaution to invest in a mosquito net.

Up to writing I haven't had a single letter, so I suppose I shall have quite a mail when I join the Battalion as I am expecting at least one or two letters from you, because before I left I told Father to write & not to wait until he heard from me here. For the present I have no more news so will close. Remember me to everybody, hoping you are both keeping fit.

I remain
With Love
Jack

Monday June 5 1916

My Dear Mother & Father,

I hope you're keeping cheery & chirpy. I can tell you I am feeling far more chirpy than I did this time last year. I don't suppose you have overlooked that fact that yesterday was the Anniversary of our famous show on Gallipoli.

I am now back with the Battalion, arriving here the day before yesterday, & really it felt like coming home. Baty is still going strong & looks absolutely fit. I had quite a decent time at Alexandria.

When at Khartoum I used to think I knew something about Desert life, but since arriving here I've altered my opinion slightly. We are miles away on the Desert, there isn't even a native mud village here, nothing but our Camp as far as the eye can see. I arrived here with a few men who came along with me in a blinding sandstorm. It took us an awful time plodding along the sand, but eventually we arrived just as it was getting dusk, and the reception I got was quite worth the journey. The temperature here is about 85° in the shade, not so high as

Khartoum but only having tents we feel it more. Although we are so far out of the World we have quite a decent Mess here & the mails, from all accounts, arrive pretty frequently. Of course we have a daily service with the Camel Corps bringing stores, water etc, so taking things on the whole we might be labouring under much worse conditions.

Baty sends his kind regards. I am enclosing one or two photographs, my first attempt with my new camera. They are rather small but I can have any of them enlarged. Good-bye for the present, give my regards to all.

I remain
Your Son
Jack

PS I sent Innes a cheque from Alex_ & told him to send the receipt to Arnwood.

June 18 1916

Being Sunday I will drop you a few lines. I must admit that since I have returned I've not been overwhelmed with letters. It is now over a month ago since I landed in this country, and so far I've received three letters.

I don't think I have told you but now I am attached to D Company with Capt. Higham as O.C. and Capt. Norbury as Second-in-Command; rather a coincidence is it not, going back to the Company. I was very pleased to see that most of the old boys have been promoted to the rank of N.C.O.

For the present do not trouble about sending parcels, as I think I am quite right in saying we shall *not* be here much longer.

How about the Naval Engagement & the Russian Advance ? Things seem to be brightening somewhat.

Just outside the Mess the C. of E. Service is taking place, but hearing that there would be a Non-Conformist Parade this morning at 9 o'clock I had decided to attend it. The Padres have quite a busy time out here on a Sunday. This outpost has been named Ashton. The Padre usually rides up from the Brigade H.Q's on Saturday evening; he has to wait until the heat of the day is over, and yet must get here before the daylight fails or be hopelessly lost. He usually arrives before dinner, stays the night, has an early Service on the Sunday Morning (also a Communion Service) afterwards partaking of breakfast, then before the sun has baked the sand, he rides over to Oldham, which is another outpost several miles away, so you see they have rather a busy day on Sunday.

The other night we gave a little sketch for the amusement of the men. Major Hurst[†] wrote two comedies & we rigged up a fine stage which the Major called the Ashton Alhambra[‡]. We had bills printed (by hand) & distributed them round the Camp, and it went off tip-top. I have no more news for the present. Baty sends his love. Remember me to all.

June 23 1916

At last I have mustered enough energy to start this letter. I have left Ashton and the Batt_ are leaving any day now. My present abode is ''Railhead''. I must explain that a small railway has been made which runs for several miles into the Desert & this place is the terminus. Rations etc which come by rail up to here, are transferred here to camels which take them on to Ashton & the other posts.

With the Battalion moving, naturally all the Stores, tents & kit-bags have to be moved, so an Officer & a draft of men had to be at the other end to unload the camels as they arrived, and to send the things per rail as the train came along. I was detailed for this job, so four days ago my little lot of 25 men left Ashton, and only for the heat we have nothing to complain of. The convoy of camels arrives about 8 o'clock AM and another convoy about 6 PM when the men fall in & set to work unloading. Then there are two trains per day, morning & evening; providing there is a wagon for us we load up & the train conveys them to the far end when the other baggage party deal with it.

[†]Major Hertz. The Manchester Evening News reported on May 6th 1915, that people were changing their names if they sounded unpleasant in English ears. Hertz published his book under his anglicised name.
[‡]The Ashton Alhambra opened on 20 May 1916 (The Manchester Sentry).

Although there are only a few of us here I like it immensely as I am absolutely on my own and have not to ask about half a dozen people before I do a thing; of course naturally if anything goes wrong I should be responsible, but common sense is the only thing required. Then again I have plenty of visitors, because anybody who goes to Suez, Alexandria or any other civilised town (from the various posts) has to entrain here, having camelled it so far, and during my stay here I have had two or three Officers to breakfast every morning (Officers who have been going to H.Q's or somewhere else on duty). They always come in the morning & wait in my tent until the 8 o'clock train goes.

The train is absolutely the last word in comfort & luxury. I went down in it yesterday for an hour or so just to have a dip in the Canal. Seats are unheard-of luxuries, the trucks are similar to open cattle trucks, so in you jump & sit on the first thing you come across, usually a nice hard wooden box which becomes no softer with the bumping of the train.

In the cool of the evening I have ridden over once or twice to Ashton just to see how things are. It was awfully funny the day I left, I had a camel sent up for me, so Baty & a few others came to see me off. In the first case the camel which was intended for me showed its teeth and began snorting on our approach. As soon as I got on its back, before I was ready, it jumped & nearly threw me over its head, much to the amusement of Baty & Co., however it did not & I arrived here quite intact, more by good luck than anything else. It was the first time I have ever been on a camel & I had not enquired into their little tricks as much as I might have done. Speaking candidly I felt very relieved on arriving safely.

Have just heard that the Batt_ is moving tonight so I shall not be here for more than a couple of days at the most. If I manage to get all the baggage down earlier I shall join the Batt_ earlier. The great discomfort here is the heat: yesterday it was 127° inside the tent, so you can form your own idea as to what it was like outside. I cannot definitely say where we are bound for, but I do not think it will be out of this country. Remember me all round.

I remain
Your Son
Jack

PS. I have dropped on quite a good chap for my servant. One of the old boys of D Coy. He is quite a young lad but looks after me like a Father.

June 30 1916

I received two letters from you last week when we were on the move. As you know this last two years I have travelled a bit & not always under the best conditions, but our journey here has beaten all my past records.

We came the whole way (about 70 miles) in open cattle trucks, & every time the train stopped & started we were thrust violently against the fellow on our left & right. I think the most annoying episode was when I had just opened a tin of pears (which I had bought from the Canteen so that I should not starve on the journey) & the train suddenly stopped, the whole bag of tricks was jerked out of my hand & the last I saw of the tin it was waltzing over the side of the truck, so I wiped the juice out of my eyes (we all had a shower of pear juice) & opened another from my reserve stock; on these journeys I have always found it advisable to have a reserve stock when possible in your haversack.

Having been on the move for a whole week I'm pleased to say that now we are settled down, arriving here at 6 o'clock this morning. I cannot tell you the exact position but our Company are at *Hill 40*, one of the Posts†. The Battalion is split up, each Company being at a different post, these posts being several miles apart. I don't suppose I shall see Baty for a week or so as his Company are not here. Only for this, I don't mind how long we are here as it is by far the best place we have been in since I rejoined. I have a tent all on my own with a table & straw matting on the floor; these two last pieces of furniture I picked up here as soon as we arrived; there is nothing like keeping one's eyes open on arriving at a new camp, and now I am jolly comfortably fixed up.

Barratt has gone home on one month's furlough. He will be calling at the Office to see Father. The cigarette case which Mr & Mrs Brooks gave me on my 21st I brought out in

---

†"D" Company were at Hill 40 in a reserve position under the command of Captain Higham supported by Capt. Townson, 2nd Lt's Grey-Burn, G.W.F. Franklin, Ross Bain, Gresty, Morten and R.J.R. Baker. The work of transport was divided between Capt Ward-Jones and 2nd-Lt M. Norbury. - The Seventh Manchesters, Captain S.J. Wilson.

mistake, so Barratt is taking it to the Office, so when Father brings it home will you put it in the box in the wash-stand cupboard in my bedroom. Major Hertz is also on his way home on furlough.

By the way, after thinking over things very seriously I have come to the conclusion that it would be quite a sound scheme if you will kindly carry on with the good work of sending a parcel periodically. The things which I most desire are: chocolate biscuits, lemon roll, Slades home-made toffee and small tins of thick cream (I can buy tinned fruits here).

The last time I was out I repeatedly asked you to send me a photo & I have come out again without one. So will you & Father be taken (*not an amateur*) & send one out in a plain wooden frame so that I can have it on my table, & if there is one left send me one of my own. Has Innes sent you a receipt as I sent him a cheque from Alexandria.

Sunday July 9 1916

My Dear Mother,

I was awfully pleased on opening your letter of a few days ago to find your photograph. It was rather a coincidence as only the day previously I had sent you the letter in which I asked you for one; however this will suffice until you & Father have one taken together.

This morning we had a most unique Church Parade; as you know there is only our Company at this Post. The Battalion Padre being several miles away, we decided to have a Parade on our own, so Capt Higham (O.C. Company) read the prayers, one of the Subalterns read the lesson and another Sub gave the sermon.

I'm awfully sorry to inform you that the old Colonel has left us today (time expired) so we do not know what is in store for us; we shall do well if we get one to equal the old Colonel. He was a typical "Old English Country Gentleman" and nowadays there are very few about. I'm hoping that Major Hertz is given command of the Battalion, he certainly ought to but one never knows what they will do in the Army.

There has just been a mail in & I'm pleased to say that I received three letters (my largest mail since I have returned), one from Father, one from you and one from one of my old stable companions at Whitley (by name Jenkins). You might send out to me the Times, the Advertiser and any other paper which has any special news in at any time. I am writing this letter to wish you "A Jolly Good Old Birthday and Many Happy Returns", according to my reckoning it should reach you about the date. I'm sorry my remembrance is confined to good wishes only but out on the Desert it is impossible to convey my congratulations in a more concrete form, however as soon as I reach civilisation I will be able to pick up some little memento from the East.

By this last mail I have received your letter with the newspaper cutting about R. Wolfenden, jolly good isn't it? I think I know the fellow who Mrs G_ told you about. I don't know why he should say such nice things about me as I never had very many dealings with him except when we played cards, then I invariably took money off him. It is funny, but he was about the luckiest fellow I have ever come across at cards. At Whitley we used to play Vingt-et-Un[†] and whenever he joined it was a foregone conclusion that he would take the *dibs*, but strange to say my luck downed him on several occasions. However he always lost in a sportsmanlike manner, and evidently he thinks no less of me having said such pleasant things about me. I have dotted his name down in my pocket book so that I can stand him a drink on the first opportune occasion; it's quite worth it, don't you think?

I am now in Command of a Platoon, and I say this without prejudice, it's the best in the Company. The first three days I had it, the O.C. Company, on his line inspection, congratulated me on the neatness & cleanliness of the lines.

I had rather a busy day yesterday, I was the Orderly Officer. I had to get up & start my duties at 3.15 AM and did not finish until 11.30 PM when I retired for my well earned night's repose.

I have not seen Baty now for about two weeks but I believe he is in the pink. According to rumour there has been an advance in France. Of course we have not got any particulars yet but hope to in a day or so. Kind regards to all, best love to yourselves. By the way, has Father removed from Piccadilly yet, if not I should like to know his reason.

Sunday July 16 1916

Dear Katie & Lilly,

I hope you are both very chirpy. I can tell you at the present time I am not feeling too chirpy; I have nothing to complain of as far as health goes, but the thing which I don't altogether relish in my present job is being caged up.

Since I wrote home I have moved, so if you see any of them you will be able to give them a bit of fresh news. At the present moment I am in Command of one of the Empire's Outposts (bow-wow). I have about 100 men & a Subaltern & here we are miles away from any other civilised being, living in a space about 300 sq yards surrounded by barbed wire.

Occasionally we have a visit in the early morning, but for three days the only outsiders seen

[†]Vingt-et-Un - the card game, Pontoon.

are the bipeds who come along with water & rations camels; the reason I refer to them as bipeds is to distinguish them from the camels, but these natives are animals with the frame of a human being.

I had a message by signal from Baty saying he was coming to have a chin-wag today, so I expect he will be here in the cool of the evening. He is about 2 miles away with the H.Q's so of course he has the chance of riding round as there are about 16 Officers there.

I have just finished my afternoon "Hate" which relieves my feelings somewhat; it consisted of strafing the numerous files which congregate in our so-called Mess and I usually devote one hour to this. The morning Hate is usually conducted by my Junior Partner. The two of us sleep in a tent and live in the Mess which is a model of modern architecture and was made in about one hour. It is made of wooden posts with straw matting for the walls & also for the roof. I will let you have a photograph of it as soon as I can get them developed.

I hope your Father & Mother are A1, begging their pardon, I should say Granny & Grandpa. Kind regards to Great Moor, Woodsmoor & the little Moors, remember me to your Aunties.

I remain
Yours sincerely
Jack

PS I shall never patronise zoos again as I have a fellow feeling for anything caged up.

July 25th 1916

Just a few hurried lines, we are on the move again plodding over the Desert. Thanks for the M/c Guardian. I suppose you are now sending the papers regularly. I also mentioned in one of my previous letters that you could carry on the good work of sending parcels, so I am living in anticipation. Yesterday Baty & myself sent in applications to join the "Royal Flying Corps" and we are now eagerly waiting to hear whether we have been accepted or not. I don't think I have any more news, and even if I had, I have not the time to write, so Au Revoir.

July 26th 1916

Dear Pat & Tom,

I am writing these few lines very hurriedly as it may be a week or two before I have the opportunity again (something doing), you needn't alarm them at home as I am saying nothing about it to them. From all accounts the hospitals are pretty full in Manchester.

135

Recently we've had some ripping news from France, fairly got the Huns on the run, haven't we? Of course if you don't hear from me regularly you must carry on with your letters & in future don't write such beastly short ones.

The next time I write there may be a fresh address on, as Baty & myself sent in our applications yesterday to join the "Royal Flying Corps" and we are now anxious waiting to hear the results. I hope we get through as I am very fed up with foot slogging over the Desert. Remember me to the usual crowd. Baty sends his kind regards.

Friday August 11 1916

I have just received Father's letter of July 22nd in which he tells me that he has seen Major Hertz.

This last week we have fairly gone through it, no doubt the papers will have told you about the glorious defeat of the Turks here; I cannot tell you more except that it was a grand sight, and to anyone who had been on the Peninsular the spectacle of batches of prisoners & the enemy retreating in disorder was doubly impressive; the one thought foremost in one's mind was that here was a chance of getting our own back & avenging the loss of the boys who are now lying buried on Gallipoli.

Then of course it is quite different from trench warfare, where as soon as your head comes above the parapet ten-to-one a piece of lead finds a billet in it. Here it is the old fashioned fighting known as "Guerrilla Warfare" and a man stands a much more sporting chance than he does with scientific trench fighting.

I cannot tell you where we are except that we are right in the heart of the Desert bivouacked in a Palm Grove. We commenced our trek on Friday August 4th. We travelled per cattle truck from C to P, about 6 miles, had half an hour's rest, a scrap of lunch, then the fun commenced. We marched off in columns of fours under cover for about four miles when we came into the open in sight of the enemy. Here we extended into lines of Companies in open order. In front of us were the Cavalry who charged, with us following up as supports. The enemy were dug in at the foot of a hill, and to see them scampering up the hill with our Cavalry at their heels was a sight never to be forgotten.

This was about midday and we followed them up until 7 o'clock PM, which was no light matter over the soft sand; if it had not been for the cheery sight of batch upon batch of prisoners which we passed, I doubt if we could have stuck it.

At last we bivouacked for the night & having placed the sentries we got down for the night. The next day, August 5th we started off at daybreak, each man having only one pint of water for the journey, so you can imagine how sparingly we sipped it as we had no idea when we should get another issue. It was a cruel march, but at last we reached our destination where we stayed the night.

Now we come to the final & worst day, Sunday August 6th. We marched off at 4 AM; it was a scorching day and before we had covered half the distance practically every man had drained his water bottle. About a mile and a half from our destination we halted & rested in a small Oasis and here the fellows, absolutely parched, began to dig for water which they found about three feet below the surface, but imagine our disappointment, on tasting it we found it to be salt water which increased one's thirst. Now we come to get on the move again (those who could stand & stagger along). Thank goodness it was only a mile and knowing there was water at the end of it, we made a special effort & at last reached it, and have been there ever since doing Outpost duty.

I have said all there is to say, but in conclusion I might add that I don't think you will hear from me quite so regularly, as there is no possible way of getting the letters away, and it is quite possible that we are going further forward, but you need not worry yourselves as I'm in the best of health & keeping my pecker up, in fact my appetite has increased. Remember me to the usual.

---

22 Aug 1916

No doubt you are anxiously awaiting this letter as I don't think I have kept you so long without dropping a line, but what with moving about & the difficulties in the line of communications with the civilised World, you must not expect to hear from me quite so regularly; then again, before writing this I've had to waste about 10 minutes trying to borrow the material to write on.

Since last writing there have been great changes in the Battalion: we have a fresh Commanding Officer & Second-in-Command. I am now 2nd-in-Command of D Coy as Capt Higham has had to go into hospital. The other day I saw Lindley Henshaw, he is now with the Fusiliers. I was very cut up when I heard of "Tim's" sudden end. The photo of myself has not yet arrived but that does not matter so much as long as yours arrives intact. I can tell you the parcel was very welcome, it could not have arrived at a better time. We were at "Katia" the Oasis where we bivouacked after our long Desert & fasting (from necessity & not from choice) trek. It arrived on the Sunday morning so we gave up the day in order to attend to it & it had our full attention, so much so that the following day it was a thing of the past.

I am awfully glad that Malcolm sent you a photo of Major Staveacre. When I come home I shall claim it. This last month or so has made one realise what a loss to the 7th the death of Major Staveacre was.

Your second parcel has just arrived. By the last mail I had letters from Mrs Green, J Brooks & a few others. You might thank Mr Brooks & tell him I will drop a line at the earliest opportunity. Although things are very quiet here now we are kept very busy. I cannot say exactly where I am, but you will have seen the name in the papers rather frequently in connection with the recent scrap here.

Aug 28 1916
Romania

Have just heard that a Mail leaves for England at 9 o'clock AM so I am taking the opportunity of letting you know that I am in the pink. I am not writing much as I have not the time but will endeavour to make up for it in my next letter. I had quite a long letter from Mr Brooks about a week ago. We have just heard that Rumania have come in, so it should not be very long now before the end. I hope you are keeping well & having some good weekends away from home. Remember me to the usual.

Sunday Sept 3 1916

I hope you are both quite well as this letter leaves me A1, although there is quite a lot of sickness about, chiefly diarrhoea.

At present we are at Romani, in fact we have been here since our little scrap. We are having quite a busy time doing a little training, and it is no easy matter marching on the soft sand. At the present time I am Acting O.C. of the Company as the O.C. and 2nd-in-Command are both sick.

Yesterday we had a Brigade march for several miles across the Desert, and being O.C. Coy. I was mounted on a horse, so did not feel quite so dejected on our arrival back in Camp as I usually feel after these *stunts* (a new word, very frequently used in this part of the World).

The other day we marched about six miles and had a dip in the Mediterranean, afterwards bivouacking for the night on the shore and returning to the Camp at sunrise the following day.

On arrival a very funny sight met our eyes, the shore was absolutely swarming with huge crabs, but immediately we appeared they scampered back into the sea. At first we did not think it such a healthy spot bathing alongside these uncanny creatures, but after having walked so far we did not like to be done out of our bathe, so in we plunged and marvellous to say, nobody was bitten. I was awfully refreshed & it was quite worth the risk.

This morning I attended the Non-Conformist Church Parade. The Non-Con Padre attached to our Brigade is a United Methodist, his name is Davy.

The flies here are nearly as bad as they were on the Peninsular. The other night we had quite a good concert. They had me down on the programme but seeing as our C.O. & the Brigade Major were present I retired discreetly.

I'm sorry I have not been able to send any more photographs but my camera has suffered like most of them, having got sand in the works, so at present it is in Port Said being repaired. You have not yet answered my question as to whether Father is still at Piccadilly spending a quid to make 10/-.

The War Office seems to have been struck with an idea of economising so have decided to take it out of us. They have already taken 2/- a day off us and I believe they are going to cut it down still more, so much so that it will mean a difference of 25/- a week to we poor Subs. What about the munition workers? I know the *poor* hard worked chaps have in their generosity decided to forego their holidays; what a *sacrifice* for those able bodied *young* men. I am going now for a canter over the Desert so Au Revoir. Remember me to the usual. You might send out about 300 Woodbines every 2 weeks for the men in my Platoon. Crossdale can get them duty-free for sending out abroad.

Sept 12 1916

Just a line or so now I have the time. We have again moved further into the Desert and are living like snails under blanket bivouacs. They are quite comfortable only one cannot possibly stand upright in them so we have to crawl in & out of them.

I am really very sorry to say that so far nothing has happened re my Flying Corps application, so I will have to carry on on foot. Now Rumania has come in I think the War should be over this year. I hope so as I'm just about fed up with being battered about from pillar to post.

The Battalion is not the same, there are only two of the original Officers left. Major Hertz is not coming back, and as you know, the old Colonel has left, and I've come to the conclusion that the sooner we leave this blighted land, whether for France, Salonika or England, the better.

Blanket bivouacs

I was rather surprised to hear that Breton had gone to France & I wish him luck; when all is said & done I would not mind a short time there myself; that is where the War will end, and there one can have a chance of revenge on our real enemy "The Hun", but as Asquith says "We will have to wait & see".

I was surprised to hear that Captain Smedley's engagement is off, do you know any particulars? He is not with us now but has got an appointment in the Sudan. I don't believe that Phyllis P_ was engaged to F. Brooks. There is nothing to write about but I thought I would let you know that I'm in the pink. Hoping you are both very well

PS. Is Father still encouraging that little Jew Adler to correspond, or has he choked him off yet? I sincerely hope so. When I look at the casualty lists I feel more than ever that the whole lot ought to be stamped out, like the natives here kill every snake they see. You might impress it on Father that if there had not been any Huns in existence I should have been living peaceably at Arnwood.

continued

Have just received your letter dated August 28th so before posting this one I thought I would tell you, also the third parcel has just arrived, so I am looking more on the bright side now than I was when I wrote the letter. I'm sorry to see that Ronald Wolfenden has died, and am very sorry to hear about S Richardson's loss.

Sunday Sept 17 1916

Just a few lines now I have a few hours leisure. At present there are only three Officers in the Company so we are living together under a blanket shelter into which we have to crawl, not being a very lofty dwelling.

I am the President of our small but happy Mess. The other day we celebrated Capt. Higham's birthday. So Baker (the other Sub) & myself thought we would spring a surprise on him. I am enclosing a Menu which I hope you will keep. It is signed by the four of us who were present. I will try to describe it: the end word of each course is the name of the various Oases in which we were bivouacked during our Desert Campaign (one way of letting you know where we have been, is it not). Now to run through the courses:

No 1. Made from OXO cubes

2. Tinned lobster

3. Tinned chicken (which B had in a parcel from home) served up with peas which we buy from the Canteen.

4. Ration beef served up with beans & roast potatoes from canteen

5. Pears & cream

6. Gingerbread (out of a parcel)

7. Savoury, sardines on toast

8. Coffee

So I think you will agree with me when I say that it reflected great credit on the *Mess President* & his staff to serve up an eight course dinner in the heart of the Desert with no proper facilities for cooking, nothing but a tin and a fire made from brushwood. I can tell you the Capt. was delighted. Also bear in mind that this 1st Class dinner was served up under our blanket shelter illuminated by candlelight. The only thing missing to make it into a real English celebration was the absence of "bubbly bubbly" but we drank his health in good old beer which I had managed to get up from the base.

I am also enclosing another little card which you might keep so that in my old age it will revive happy days. I received this just as I was settling down to write this. Chadwick is the O.C. of C Coy, he is one of the *very few* of the original ones left, and a few days ago he had a notification to the effect that he had received the "Order of the White Eagle" for good work in Gallipoli.

I should also like you to notice the way my name is pronounced, with the emphasis on the last syllable, as I am always telling people off for spelling my name with an 'O'.

Hope you are both in the pink, as this letter leaves me. Just heard that there is a Mail coming up today so I'm hoping to see in black & white how you are keeping. I have written to Mr Brooks, remember me to Mr & Mrs Bourne & the two cooing doves, not forgetting my old pal, Pauline.

> I remain
> With Love
> Your Son
> Jack

PS Have the Menu framed for my bedroom

———————————————————

Sept 14th. 1916.

A
Dinner
by
The Officers of "D" Company
to
Capt C.E. Higham
on
the occasion of the anniversary of his birth.

Menu.

Consommé Katia

Ecrèvisse Mayonaise à Gilban

Poalet fricassée à Pelusium

Rôsbif à l'anglais.

Pêches Pelba - El Kabah

Petits fours à l'Oghratina

Grissons conservés à l'Hod el Megiliat

Café

Wadi View Bivouac

Hod - el - Megiliat

Wine List on application to the Pess President.

Sept 21 1916

My Dear Mother,

This is in reply to your of the 6th which I received yesterday. I am pleased to say that I'm on the pink in spite of the climatic conditions. We have gone a little further inland since I last wrote to you. I have now had three parcels from you, the one you mentioned coming from Mr Horn has not yet arrived. I was rather surprised to hear that you had been honoured with a visit from Mrs H_

I've seen Lindley out here, but I have not seen Alan,

It's awfully bad luck on Mrs Harrison, is it not. Rather a strange thing happened yesterday: during our early morning parade it actually commenced to rain. Whilst it lasted it was most refreshing, but unfortunately it was only a five minute shower. Just fancy, the very first spot I have seen since leaving England. In the afternoon I killed a couple of snakes. I hope that yourself & Father are in the pink.

Thursday Sept 28 1916

Just a few lines before the mail leaves for the Old Country. I hope you are quite well and I'm pleased to hear that you are not moping away at Arnwood, but are getting away at every opportunity. At the present moment I am not feeling too pleased as there have been two mails this week and there was not a single line from anyone in any of them for me. In one of your letters you said that Mr Horn had sent me some sweets, well up to writing they have not arrived.

I think I told you that Baty went to hospital the other day; he had not been well for some time but I don't think it's anything serious, just a little run down; if only he had had a short furlough at home it would have made all the difference.

How is business? Anything doing? It's awfully difficult writing as there is nothing to write about. I'm rather afraid that my Flying Corps is a washout. According to the "War News" which we get daily, the Allies seem to be going strong, then what about Greece? It was rather good work bringing down two Zepps on the S.E. Coast was it not? I hear that several 3rd line Officers have been wounded in France. I hope that Stockport & Bury are quite well.

Oct 5 1916

Just a few lines in answer to yours of the 16th and another not dated. A few days ago we got a rumour here that Breton was killed, but from what you say I am very pleased to hear that he

The Bedouin Marquee – a considerable luxury

is only wounded; I should say that anybody who comes back from France even if wounded is jolly lucky. Mr Horn's parcel has not yet arrived.

I don't know who told you that Whitley was our Commanding Officer, but unfortunately they are mistaken as he is not even with the Battalion now. The Command has not been given to one of our own Officers. There are now only three of the originals left, another one, Capt Chadwick O.W.E., a great pal of mine, left us this morning to join the R.F.C., so last night Higham & myself gave him a farewell dinner in our Bivouac.

I think I told you that we had found an old Bedouin marquee. It is so spacious that we had twelve in for last night's farewell festivity; not a bad find, was it, when you come to think that only for our fortunate find, we should have to improvise a blanket shelter in the daytime to keep off the sun, and at night pull it down so that we could wrap our blankets round us in order to keep warm as the remainder of the Battalion do.

In Father's letter he talks about me getting another pip on my shoulder; well you can tell him from me that the few of us who are left have quite given up the idea of promotion , especially under the new regime. There is only one promotion which is worth having, and that is, when the War is over, to be promoted to a "Civilian".

I had a letter from old Baty yesterday, he is at a Convalescent Home in Cairo. I might possibly be in Alexandria when you receive this as there are a certain number of men & Officers going for a week's leave. The first party go tomorrow, but up to writing the list of

Officers is not out so I don't know whether I'm a "winner" or not, but I have a strong idea that I am.

Yesterday I had a fine canter over the Desert. Where we are at present there is no scrapping but there are quite a number of wells which require guarding extending over a pretty large area, and of course every day these guards have to be visited by an Officer, so yesterday I took on the job. I hope you are all quite well, remember me to the usual.

PS. Word has just come through that I am detailed to proceed to Alexandria tomorrow for a week, so Cheer-oh.

JCM nursing septic knees.

Union Club
Alexandria
Egypt
Oct 9th 1916

You may be surprised at receiving this letter from me or you may not, as I told you in my previous letter that I was coming here, but knowing by this time what Active Service is I never believe any good rumours of a rest, however authentic, until I am actually away from the Battalion with several miles between us, so in a way you will understand that I am rather surprised, especially when I tell you there are plenty of Officers left behind who are far more entitled to a holiday than I am, but having been detailed by the C.O. to go with the first party I had no option, so here I came, not unwillingly I may add.

According to my usual custom something extraordinary had to happen to me. I think I told you that a few days ago I had rather a good canter over the Desert – unfortunately I had not my breeches with me & I rode in shorts, with the result that after I had finished I cultivated two beautiful sores on the side of my thigh where the bare flesh had rubbed against the saddle, but I did not think they were worth troubling the M.O. with, I thought I would let them take their own course. However, this might have been all right in ordinary times, but during our two days journey here, what with marching from Camp to train, the flies having a good meal off them & the dust flying into them, they turned septic and by the time we arrived here on the 2nd day I was going through hell (to put it in soldier's language). In fact if it had not been that I was leading 50 men from our Company I could not have stuck it. However on arriving here, having fixed the men up & my own quarters, I immediately went to the Dressing Station where I went through a delightful half hour having the septic squeezed out and hot fomentations tied round. After this performance they sprung another surprise on me by telling me I must go into hospital, so here I thought it was time to speak. Up until then I had not said a word, but just let them amuse themselves pulling my legs about as though they had no connection with me, but at this stage I arose and put my foot down, so to speak, & have not gone into hospital.

With having them bandaged & poulticed every day they were practically better, but yesterday, meeting Chadwick in town who is waiting for a boat home, four of us decided to go roller skating. Not having been on a rink for about 6 years the inevitable happened & for the first ten minutes it seemed to be a competition as to who could come the biggest cropper, & of course, every time I came down the bandages on my poor old legs became looser & eventually came off, so this morning when I went to have them dressed an extra two or three sores were found to have grown on my legs. Of course they are nothing & I'm making hay while the sun shines as we have only three more days. The most annoying part of the whole thing was the first night when the Colonel asked me to dine with him at the Savoy Palace Hotel & of course I had to cry off & rest my leg, but still if I had not rested them after our two days journey I should most certainly have had two very nasty legs, but you will be pleased to hear that only for the first night they have not interfered with my pleasure at all.

Yesterday morning I had quite a spree. We paid a visit to the Ordnance Stores, buying in, spent the whole morning there, and at night when I went through my a/c I discovered I had spent £25. Of course buying such things as binoculars & wrist watches etc it soon mounts up.

Sultan Hussein Club
Alexandria
Oct 11 1916

I don't know whether you will notice but this letter was started two days ago at the Union Club & I am now finishing it at the Sultan Club where I have not had the fortune to pick up a decent pen, hence the writing. You will naturally come to the conclusion that I am having a busy time taking two days to write a letter, well I am but it's the right sort of a busy time. We are so busy enjoying ourselves that we have come to the conclusion that it would have been more of a rest if we had stayed with the Battalion. On the other hand it is a complete change to have one's food without sand in it & having breakfast in bed appeals to most of us.

I hope you are in the pink & realise that now we are top dogs, so that I may be home within twelve months, so keep your peckers up and don't be downhearted. Remember me to the usual & tell them that I am like the proverbial "illweed" still flourishing.

Oct 15 1916

I am now back again on the Desert. We arrived back at the Bivouac at 10 o'clock this morning so you will see that I have not wasted much time before dropping you a line. I must say that I've had one of the best holidays I've ever had and have come back feeling fit for anything.

I had several surprises whilst at Alex_ one day walking at the Club who should I bang into but Leslie Haws; he has got quite a decent billet in Alexandria. I'm awfully glad because I don't think he would stick it out here very long. He told me that you had met him in Caernarvon and he was awfully pleased with the parcel you sent him. You never told me about it.

Then the day before we came away I had another surprise, I received a letter from a girl saying that she had heard I was in Alexandria & that she would like to see me, would I ring her on the phone. So of course I did and arranged to see her the same afternoon at the Sporting Club. It is rather strange, but this girl is related to the Prestons of Bramhall & at Florrie Preston's 21st three years ago she was over, having just left school (Pat will remember her). She & her brother also went to the State with us on Xmas Eve. Well of course three years makes quite a difference to a girl of this age & I had not the faintest notion what she was like, so off I went to the Sporting Club. As soon as I got there I saw an awfully pretty girl having tea at a table but did not recognise her, however I took the bull by the horns so to speak, & after having feasted my eyes on her for five minutes I strolled up & asked her, & found that I was right. It was a most trying time for me because at this time of day the garden is packed with all the knuts of Alexandria & if I had gone up to the wrong one I should have felt an awful fool. To make a long tale short I had a ripping time but unfortunately this was the last day. If I discovered her before I should have gone to several dances. However she gave me a very pressing invitation to go & stay with them at the very first opportunity and I rather fancy that I shall avail myself of this invitation. I know I should have a ripping time.

My surprises did not finish here as we left our M.O. there and who should turn up as our new one but Dr Schofield. He has just come out & knowing nobody he was felling rather downhearted but he was awfully pleased to see somebody from home whom he knew. He is coming round to my tent this afternoon for tea, when I hope to give him a little of your cake; it will be rather a change, something home-made.

I expect by the time you receive this you will have had a parcel from B&Q Tawa Alexandria; they are Egyptian curio dealers so I have bought one or two things. The gong is for Pat, the vase is for yourself and the brooch is for Beatrice (21st present). I think she will like it. I gave £3 for it; not knowing the value of jewellery I don't know whether I've been done or not, but it struck me as being rather a fine piece of work. What do you think? Round the neck of the vase you will find some writing like this

This is Egyptian writing & the word it forms means "Long life" I have forgotten the word but it is some word like "Mispah". I hope Pat will like the gong.

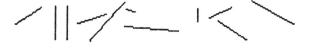

On arriving back a rather cheery sight met my gaze: there were four parcels & one letter and some papers fro me. Two of the parcels were your specialities, one was the pipe & tobacco with which I am delighted & the other one contained two 2-gross boxes of fruit caramels from Mr Horn for which I will write & thank him at the first opportunity.

I have just heard that there was a mail in, so off I dashed to the Mess & found awaiting for me your letter of Oct 1st & some letters from Father. In your letter you seem to think that my last letter to you was one of a pessimist, well perhaps so, as you know I am very changeable, especially so of late. One minute I am down in the dumps and the next I am walking on air, so-to-speak. Capt Higham is now having his rest at Alexandria so I am once again O.C. Company. I'm rather like a thermometer the way I rise & fall but still as I have so often remarked, I shall consider it quite the best promotion when I am once again a civilian. But still, the War cannot go on for so long now, so whilst I am here I will do as I have always done, my best, because there is no doubt about it, if everyone does his best it will certainly bring our task about of exterminating the Huns very much quicker.

Baty is now better & at present is having his summer holidays at Alexandria, rather unfortunate that we were not there together, still I hope he has as good a time as I had. Thank Lena for the chocolates. Remember me to the usual & tell Mr J Bourne to keep his pecker up. Dr Schofield wishes to be remembered to you.

23/10/16

I am now writing my usual Sunday epistle although I have no news whatever. By the last mail I received your letter of the 5th also a parcel. I'm awfully glad Breton is not seriously wounded, but I hope he manages to stick in England for a good while. I should think that now you will see the force of my argument when I was at home and rather impatient as you thought I was when I was so keen on coming out to Egypt again. Baty is next to me also writing home, he returned from Alexandria yesterday & is much better for a change.

On Friday I had rather a good day – the Colonel & four of us rode to --------a place on the Coast about six miles from our present camp. We had lunch there & returned in the afternoon after having had a bathe; unfortunately I was barred this pleasure on account of my septic knees. I enjoyed it thoroughly although the next day I felt rather stiff. It was rather a cheeky undertaking on my part as it is the first long ride I've been, and I had Capt Higham's horse which is the fastest one in the stable, & every time we had a canter or a gallop my old gee would insist on beating the others with the result that it took me all my time to stick on, much to the amusement of my confreres.

The second night the Doctor was with us a rather funny little episode happened. Four of us after dinner one night said we would take a walk to the Outpost, so the Doc joined us & off we started. We arrived there all right and had about an hour's chin-wag with Barratt who is there, then we started on our journey homewards. In the meantime a thick mist had come on and naturally we lost our way, and to lose one's way in this desert is something pretty awful as there are no landmarks. After roaming about for two solid hours at last we found our camp. We were absolutely wet through with perspiration & the mists which come on here pretty frequently now are awfully dense & drench one to the skin. I felt awfully sorry for poor old Schofield as it was his first voyage over the soft sand and also he had been bad all day with diarrhoea (everybody has it for the first week or so out here) so he was pretty well done when we got back although two of us had been helping him along.

By the way I do not see any possible chance of being home for Xmas so we are preparing for as good a time as possible by writing home for Xmas hampers. You say the bally old PO authorities will not accept more than a 7lb parcel. In a parcel of this size you can get as many Xmas puddings, mince pies & almonds etc as you can, but I should fancy there will be some method of sending out hampers per the Military Forwarding Officer, Plymouth, however I do not know, but ask Father to make some enquiries. I suppose turkey will be out of the question but if you send me a tinned chicken it will make quite a decent dinner for a few of us. For Xmas parcels J Marks, St Anne's Sq. is quite a good place. They have almost anything & they also pack them up & send them direct from the shop. Ask Father to get Crossdale to send me out 1000 Woodbines every three weeks or so & I will send Father a cheque on. Crossdale has them sent direct from Wills free of duty (they are for my men).

Oct 24 1916

Hearing there was a mail out at 8 o'clock in the morning I am just scribbling you a note whilst waiting for the Doctor who is coming in my tent this evening for a little chin-wag.

There was a parcel mail in today & I received the Woodbines from Crossdale. In my last letter I asked Father to send some out but apparently I must have mentioned it before, well if I had I had quite forgotten. All the same I thank him very much. By the way the pipe Father sent me is smoking beautifully, it is as sweet as a knut and has been admired times without number; also the tobacco is the very kind I wanted. Also by today's mail I received another of your special parcels. I am sending Mrs Briggs a letter by this mail as I have had a little more time for writing these last few days.

I do not know whether I told you but the last time we were on the outpost line I found a man asleep on guard. Well of course this is a most serious offence so I reported it with the result that the man was Court Marshalled & got 10 years, however it was commuted to three for which I was rather pleased.

I hope you are both well. I might say that I never in all my life felt fitter. Rather an amusing little episode happened the other day. I put the photo of myself on my table; presently my Orderly came in and after scrutinising it for several minutes, turned to me & asked if it was the photo of one of our Officers, whereon I informed him that it was myself, much to his surprise, but I have altered a little being now fatter in the face & thinner in the lower regions; of course as you know I could very well spare a little of my somewhat corpulent tummy.

The weather now is much more agreeable not being quite so hot in the middle of the day. The nights are very cold, but once I get into my flee-bag with one or two blankets on top of that I am as snug as it is possible for anyone to be.

I have not yet received the photograph of yourself & Father although about three weeks ago you said you had had it taken, so I'm relying on the old motto so well known to those at Arnwood, especially at Xmas time that "Everything comes to those who wait"

No more for the present, so Au Revoir,

November 2nd 1916

Yesterday there was a parcel mail in & I received the parcel of cigs from Crossdale also one of your specials for which I thank you very much. I had quite a good letter mail the other day including two from Constance Harrison & one from Mrs Briggs. Rather a funny coincidence, but I wrote the Mrs Briggs the other day so our letters must have crossed on the way. I am writing to Mr Horn by this mail thanking him for the two boxes of caramels he sent me.

For a few days last week I was on a job which I like, one my own with fifty men. I was on a detached post about two miles from the Battalion. I intended to do a lot a letter writing whilst there, but after being there four days I received orders to rejoin the Battalion & since then we have moved another twelve miles inland & are once again living like rabbits under blanket shelters. Whilst on the post I had a wooden shed to live in which I partitioned off, having one part for my living room which I furnished with a small home-made table covered with a brown blanket which made quite a decent looking table cloth, & on which I displayed my photographs. The other part I had for boudoir.

Whilst there the Doctor rode over & had tea with me twice. I also had one or two more visitors for afternoon tea & everybody received my cosy little home with admiration. I felt quite like a king in my two or three acres surrounded by barbed wire. I also had two cooks

for myself & anything I requested in the way of stores I wired through to the Battalion, so you can see I did not have a bad time at all. However all good things come to an end & I am now once again with the Battalion.

In this letter I am enclosing a few snaps. If you cannot make out what they are you will find a description of them on the back of each one. The flies are rather troublesome this morning. At the present time we are having ideal weather: the daytime is like a moderately hot day in Spring at home, the nights are awfully cold but knowing what to expect we dress accordingly.

Since starting this letter three days ago I have gone through quite a lot. I told you about finding a Bedouin marquee, well we have had half of it pinched, so only being half the size I have had to resort once again to living under a blanket bivouac. However I made quite a cosy one just big enough for myself. The first night I buried myself in my sleeping bag for the night; at 4 a.m. I awoke suddenly & felt something uncanny with about fifty legs creeping over my forehead. Guessing what it was I lay perfectly still until it had crawled off & heard it amongst some paper which was on the ground, then I brought my electric torch to bear on it & you can imagine my horror when I saw the largest centipede it's ever been my luck to come across. Needless to say, sleep was out of the question for the remaining hours. I was jolly glad I had wakened up instead of attempting to sweep it off in a semi-sleepy state.

The following day I changed my bivouac a few yards away. We had just finished dinner & it commenced to rain. Coming from Manchester I thought I knew what rain was, but never in all my life have I experienced rain like this: chunks of ice the size of a billiard ball came down to the accompaniment of thunder & illuminated by vivid flashes of lightning. Needless to say, myself & all my belongings were soaked, so I sought shelter in the remains of our camel-hair marquee which is occupied by Higham. The rain came through that but it was a big improvement to my own place which was blown away in the gale. After seeing that the men had some hot tea made we got down for the night about 11 o'clock, & although everything I had on was soaking & I was lying in about 6 inches of water, I slept quite soundly & felt quite fit the following morning. After I had laid out all my things to dry we were all in the same boat. This was yesterday, so I spent the rest of the morning rebuilding my house & I have certainly made it so that the gale will not blow it away again, but unfortunately I discovered last night that it was not quite watertight. Of course it is quite impossible to make it so with only having blankets.

Last night I had been in bed about four hours when another shower came on, not quite so severe as the previous night, but it was a tropical shower, enough said. In less time than it takes to write it, my flea-bag with myself inside it was soaked, so I got up, took my bed with me & again visited Higham. Luckily the rain had not penetrated through his roof this time. There were three of us now in his place, packed like herrings, so I planted down my wet flea-bag, got inside it & slept soundly for the remainder of the night, so it won't surprise you to know that after those two wet nights my nose is a little bit stuffed up & I am now wondering what tonight will bring.

The day after tomorrow I am going on a bombing course for four days when I shall be living under canvas, so I'm hoping that during those four days all the rain which is hanging around will have come down, rather a selfish wish, isn't it?

Today is Sunday & we have spent the greater part of the morning deeply interested in a rather barbarous spectacle. We caught two centipedes, put them together in a large biscuit tin & they gave us a most horrifying exhibition of a fight to the death. The victor kills the other by breaking its neck. No doubt you will think we are a bloodthirsty crowd, but little amusements of this sort break the monotony of the Desert. I remember once reading when I was a *boy* (many years ago) some historian or explorer who was keen on the Eastern life & he called it "The Call of the Desert". I can safely say that once away it will never call me back.

Before I close I must say I am delighted with the photograph, it was a speaking likeness: Father with the inimitable expression of his "laying down the law", then yourself with what Miss Wood describes as a soft mouth & your grey hair. If Father was only bald you would make quite a stately old couple. I could wager anything that Pat had a hand in doing your hair. There is only one fault: you are staring just a little – didn't the dicky bird appear at the right moment? Jesting aside I am extremely pleased with it as it is the only photo I carry in my mobile kit on these treks. Of course, these last two nights it has been soaked along with myself but it is none the worse & when all is said & done, whether is discomfort or enjoyment, three is better than one. I must now draw to a close as the Doctor is coming round to have tea with me, so Au Revoir

I remain
Your Son
Jack

PS. In places you will notice the writing is more pronounced in colour. This is owing to the rain. I felt very relieved to find that it was not all washed out.

Nov 14 1916

My Dear Mother,

This is in reply to yours of Oct 24th which I received yesterday. I was awfully sorry to hear about the death of Mr Hardman.

Since last writing I have had a few days away from the Battalion on a bombing course, then after the course was over I managed to spend a day and a half in Port Said. It is not much of a place, nothing like Alexandria, but at the same time it was quite an agreeable change. I stayed at the Casino Palace on the sea front. It is quite the most up-to-date hotel there.

When I was at home you may have heard me talk of Mr Robins who was the Rector at Khartoum Cathedral, well strange to say I met him in Port Said. He was on the ill-fated Arabia which as you know, you must have read, was torpedoed in the Mediterranean a few days ago. Fortunately all on board were saved with the exception of two engineers. Some of the passengers were picked up & taken to Malta & a good number were brought back to Port Said. With several of these I had some very interesting conversations. I might say that a few of my letters will no doubt be lying at the bottom of the sea as she was taking our mails home. I am not quite sure whether the one I wrote to Tom & Pat would be on that boat or not.

At the present moment I am suffering slightly from a little indiscretion in my past. We have a new horse in the stables which is very nervous & frightened of camels; it is very strange but horses are scared to death at the sight of a camel until they become accustomed to seeing them daily. Several of the fellows refused to ride the horse but I did, not having quite so much discretion & yesterday took it out for a ride. The fun commenced when a train came along & it started to back. The train having passed, it settled down again but refused to come over the line, so I dismounted & led it across. I then remounted, & much to my amazement a camel emerged from behind some mounds. At the same time the horse espied it, & of course the inevitable happened; it gave one snort & started off. It was absolutely frantic. I was taken by surprise or it never would have started. However we took the railway at a jump & I was just about to begin to feel that I had it in hand when it stumbled slightly. This movement sent me forward, I went over its head, did a very clever somersault in the air & came down a deuce of a bump on my back. I raised myself up & saw my horse about 50 yards away, still racing on in its frenzy, so I walked by the nearest route to my bivouac & I consider myself jolly lucky in having nothing more than a slightly sprained back. It is very slight & enables me to carry on as usual.

I am enclosing a few more snaps which I have taken.......I sent some with my last letter & by the way, from Port Said I sent you a little book of Post Cards. Let me know if you have received them. In your letter you say that you have sent me a wrist watch........I have not yet received it. I bought one in Alexandria but it is always as well to have two as they are invariably out of order with the sand getting in the works. In your letter you do not say whether you have received the mementos I sent from Alexandria or not. Hoping you are both in the pink of condition.

Nov 28th 1916

My Dear Mother & Father,

Just a few lines to remind you that I have not quite forgotten you although rather a long period has elapsed since I last wrote.

In your last letter you mentioned several people. Joe Chatterton is now back with us I'm pleased to say. Whitley, Woodward & Capt Ward-Jones are not with us now on the staff & the last two are with the Brigade.

The way you are spending Xmas this year will be quite a novelty for both yourself & Father & I hope it will be the last Xmas you will be so scattered about. Tell Pat that the next time she had better time it better & not upset folks at such a festive time. The time is drawing near & I sincerely hope that you will have as jolly a Xmas as possible. You might tell Father that this is the last Xmas that he will be able to kid himself on being a young man, so he had better make the best of the short time because when he attains the honourable position of *Grandpa* he will have to settle down & of course the same applies to yourself. It won't be a case of Mr & Mrs Charles Stanley going to dinner etc, but Grandma & Grandpa going to the weekly concerts of the old people in the park. Then of course in a few years (a few weeks in this case I hope) the soldier son returns to find he is now an Uncle and devoted the remainder of his time between training the youngster and taking out the dear old white-haired Grandparents. Rather a good story, isn't it?

By the way, how much money have I now invested, & what in? Tell Father he can invest another £100 for me & I will let him have a cheque, & I don't want any of your safe concerns giving 2.5% but something which gives 5% as soon as he can because it is simply lying idle where it is.

We have just finished in inter-platoon football competition & I cannot tell you how pleased I am that my platoon went right through & won the final yesterday. I hope you have got all the snapshots & also the parcel I sent from Alexandria.

Dec 5th 1916

Just a few lines to wish you the very best of luck, prosperity & happiness in the New Year.

At the present moment I am not with the Battalion but on a special job which is rather an unpleasant one, although I must say it is quite the softest & cushiest job I have yet struck in the Army as it exempts me from parades & marching. At the present time the Battalion is on trek, or in other words a four day march & in the ordinary course of events I should also have been marching, but I came by train which I to my way of thinking is quite the best way of getting here. To make a long story short, I am charge of an Officer who is under close arrest, & everywhere he goes, I go. At night I am supposed to sleep with one eye open in case he takes it into his head to hop-it, to use a slang phrase. Under ordinary conditions I should be at this hour in dreamland, but he having a bit of writing to do before his Court Martial which comes off tomorrow morning early, I have decided to write this letter in order to prevent me from falling asleep.

Your parcel arrived today & I must say it was an absolute Godsend. As I have previously stated we came here by train, the Battalion having not yet arrived, so we are living with various Units & I received your parcel by calling at the Station where I had left instructions for it to be sent. It was about 1.30 pm & we had had nothing since our breakfast at 6.30 am. We had been traipsing about the Desert the whole time looking up various people & I can tell you, the shortbread & lemon roll soon disappeared. Where we are is such a desolate hole that if it had not been for that parcel we should have had nothing until 8.30 in the evening. By the way, why on earth don't you send the parcels as you used to, in a fairly strong box; & if the Postal Authorities object, take it to some other Post Office, as fellows out here get parcels in the same kind of biscuit tin box that you used to send mine in, & I'm sure if they can get them, there is a peculiar kind of order of their own governing the Stockport Post Officers. Your parcel I received today was nearly coming in two parts when I received it, although luckily the contents were quite intact, but nevertheless if you can pack them up in the original way, do so. I am so glad that the parcel has arrived from Alexandria & that you like the contents.

Although yourself & Beatrice have acknowledged receipt of same, up to writing I have not received any word from Bury as to whether they like the gong or not.

I am awfully pleased to hear that Jack Richardson has at last got his Commission. When you see him give him my best congratulations.

When I was at home, as you know, quite a few of the Fair Sex promised to knit me socks – well I foolishly thought they meant it, with the result that I am now practically sockless as there are no such things as hosiers on the Desert, & relying on their promises I did not buy any whilst I was in Alexandria. Still it is my own fault; I might have known it is a case of out of sight, out of mind with most people nowadays.

I don't know whether I told you but Dick is now in South Africa. I had a letter from his girl who by the way he is now officially engaged to, & she informed me. About six months ago I had a letter from Pat asking me to let her know what I would like & she would be delighted to send it. Well, in reply I made a very modest request that she should send me a little home-made lemon cheese. Since then I have heard a great deal about this lemon cheese in letters, but up to writing I have seen nothing of it in parcels, so you might tell her not to worry about it as I would not like to be the cause of any inconvenience to her daily duties which must be numerous, considering there are two of them.

From all accounts you are having pretty severe weather now in England. Of course the weather here is supposed to be pretty severe by the Natives, but we find it quite agreeable except for the occasional showers which are few & far between, thank goodness. The daytime is like English hot summers but at night it becomes awfully cold & there is rather a lot of heavy dew, but this being the case every night we know what to expect & make the necessary preparations.

In one of your letters you mentioned about my body belt. I might say that I never wear one now & have not since I returned to this ancient & Biblical land, in fact I gave them both away some time ago to a chap who was troubled with pains in his Little Mary. In a way, where we are now is somewhere that the Children of Israel wandered, then in later years Napoleon came when he attacked El Arish. Personally I think that to trek to this God-forsaken land in the bygone days when there were no such things as tinned essentials & luxuries that we get, it was a far greater feat than now, although when you consider the state of civilisation then & now I don't know whether it was, but whether it was or not I shall be quite prepared to evacuate the land of sand & sun at any moment I am ordered.

I hope I am not boring you with this detailed piffle but I must do something to keep awake.

Saturday Dec 16th 1916

It is very near Xmas Day now. When you receive this it will be over & I hope that you had the usual jolly time. I cannot say where we shall spend the day but from the look of things I think it will not be in the way one would spend it from choice.

The lemon cheese arrived a week ago & I cannot find words to express what a huge success it was. You can class it with the lemon roll & soda cake. So far, up to writing, none of my Xmas parcels has arrived but I am not at all sorry as several of the other Officer's have, so we have quite enough to be going on with. Already we have had four Xmas puddings & I have enough in stock to serve up every night for dinner for another week, and mine will arrive most likely when we have finished the present stock so they will be quite in time.

As you know I'm the Company's Mess President & all Officers' parcels etc are at my disposal & in safe keeping, so when I allude to my stock you will know what I mean. I cannot tell you exactly where we are, no doubt you will read in the daily papers before the month is out, but I can tell you that we are more than a hundred miles from any civilised place. We are now living à la Gallipoli in dug-outs against enemy aircraft. For the Mess we have a large dug-out with the camel-hair stuff as a roof & I must say that it is jolly comfortable & quite warm. We have dinner at night; the place is illuminated with candles & we all sit around on the floor Gypo fashion (something like a tailor sits). We have great doings when Xmas pudding comes on. We soak it with whisky (brandy not being available) then light it, after which it is devoured by the hungry mortals.

I received a letter from you yesterday dated Sept 24th. I don't know where it can have been all the time. In it you ask what my pay is now, it is somewhere about twelve & sixpence a day. We do not live entirely on Army rations but I get stores up from Cairo & other places every so often......such things as sauces, cheeses etc & we pay 2/- per day..Of course this does not include drinks which are the most costly things in the Mess. A bottle of beer costs 1/3, a bottle of soda water 10d, so you see it is rather a costly thing to have a thirst here.

Where we are now is rather nice as we have very little time on our own, but I don't suppose we shall be here long as the last month we have been continually on the move, never staying in one place more than a couple of days & it takes me that long to get really comfortable & to make a proper dug-out.

Boxing Day 1916

Just a few lines in my spare time. Although we have just had two days holiday to celebrate Xmas I have not had quite so much spare time as one would imagine, hence this short missive.

At these festive times, as you know, there are some poor blighters who work overtime to provide the necessaries which Little Mary rebels against. This year, being the *Mess President,* I've had quite a busy time: the whole of Xmas morning I was scouting the Desert for our turkey & other Xmas tit-bits, which I might say proved to be quite a fruitless journey. I am enclosing our menu – you might think this is a delusion on my part & it certainly sounds rather mythical to have such a spread 80 miles away on the Desert, but everything down on the menu we had.

Some days beforehand I had written to Cairo ordering a fresh turkey three-quarters cooked to be sent, and this bird gave me endless worry & trouble by not turning up in time, but much to my surprise it has arrived whilst I'm writing this letter, so we are having another Xmas dinner this evening. Last night's dinner was not without turkey although one did not turn up, as from the various Xmas parcels we managed to rake up four tinned turkeys which were jolly good. We also had Champagne & port sent up from Cairo. Dinner being over we had the usual toasts then went & had a look at the men who were having an open air concert round a huge camp fire. Each of us gave a little speech wishing them the old wish, then Baker & myself gave a turn in the form of a duet with a good chorus in which they all joined in. We then bade them Good night & retired to the Harem to finish our evening in the Mess.

After dinner Bateman & Chatterton & a few others came round to our Mess & we had quite a good old Xmas jollification breaking up in the early hours of this morning. The parcel of cigs came in time & I was awfully pleased at being able to have them distributed to my platoon Xmas morning. I was more pleased to have the cigs in time than I was at getting the other parcels which all arrived at the same time & I thank you very much. The contents were fine & they were typically Xmas parcels. I also had an awfully nice cake & some cigars from Rivelyn & I must confess that I could not have had a nicer time anywhere except at Arnwood. I hope you had a good time. I must now close as it is not the best position for writing to be sat in a dug-out using one's knees for a table with a candle for an illuminant. The best of wishes for the New Year to all of you. This also includes the latest addition to the family which I presume has arrived.

Your Son
Jack (Mizpah)

The menu card is written & designed by one of the men in my platoon. Is it not awfully well done? The names down the sides are the names of places we have visited in our Desert trek.

Jan 8th 1917

My Dear Father,

This is in reply to yours of Dec 13th in which you mention the large sum of money which I think will be far more remunerative out of Cox & Co., so I herewith enclose a cheque for

£100. I suppose now the War is at full swing it is hardly the time for speculation, so I quite agree with you that it is quite the best thing to put it with my other investment & receive a modest 5%.

No doubt you will think this writing is worse than usual, so it is, but this morning I have had two of my finger-ends lanced with the result that I cannot wield my pencil with such a grace of ease and cannot put in my clever flourishes.

I don't know whether any letters were posted to me from the 18th Dec to the 24th Dec but if so they will be rather wet by now as we have received information that letters posted on that date have been sunk. I suppose it is looked upon as a huge practical Xmas joke by Bruno & his fellow countrymen. I may have a pleasant surprise for you in a short time which if it comes off will mean a slight alteration in the address of my correspondence. I received another parcel from Mother the other day containing mince pies & lemon roll. I think it would be No.1 but owing to my impetuosity & impatience to see the contents I threw the wrapper away without seeing the number on it, but I'll look in future. I've also had a tin of cigarettes from Dick's girl & a very useful parcel from the Chapel. You might thank them for it although at the first opportunity I will write them myself. I hope you are all well & that everything went off without a hitch at Milner Avenue†. No more for the present. Wishing you a Happy New Year etc.

I remain
Your Son
Jack

PS. In future address my letters to the Batt_

There are no letters and no indications as to his whereabouts between January and May 1917. The 7th Manchesters advanced through Romani to El Arish, then in February they were transferred to France. They sailed on the "Kalyan" from Alexandria on March 3rd 1917 and landed at Marseilles marching via Orange, Lyon, Chalon-sur-Saone, Dijon, Paris, Juvissy & Amiens. The extra equipment they were given were a short Lee Enfield, a tin hat and a respirator. They were very cold.

He had obviously been home on leave before the next set of letters was written.

---

†On January 6th at 5, Milner Avenue, Bury: to Mr & Mrs T.V. Hardman neé Pattie Morten, a son.

FRANCE

May 28th 1917
France

My dear Pat,

You will be surprised to hear that I'm on the move again. Once more I am rejoining the Battalion who are at present in the line so the next letter you receive from me will be in the dim future probably, however these moves break the monotony & in about three weeks I expect to be home. How is Tom -still busy I presume. I hear that P.N. received my Xmas card, but her excuse for not acknowledging was not knowing my address, rather a frail one isn't it, as if she didn't, anyone would have told her. However if she does not care to correspond it's quite all right to me. I'm not in the habit of begging & praying people to correspond & I'm not going to start now *at my time of life* not even to **Miss P.N**†.

France
May 30th 1917

My dear Pat,

This is in reply to yours of May 13th just received; it has been all over France following me about. Pleased to hear about Sam Howarth's promotion. You may be reading about your brother in some daily paper as tomorrow I'm rejoining the Battalion who are in the line so I'm just scribbling off a few letters whilst I've the time. I can't grumble at all as I've had a fairly cushy time so far & I hope to be home very shortly now. John Ronald seems to have a mind of his own. I rather fancy you are spoiling him. Of course poor old Tom had all the spirit knocked out of him before J.R.‡ appeared on the scene, I suppose. When I think of Tom I always think of that cheap blood which used to appear at the Royal, "Is Marriage a Failure". Isn't the weather topping now? Just the kind for leave, isn't it? Well no more for the present.

France
Sunday June 24 1917

It is quite a week since I had the opportunity of writing to you, but as I expected when I rejoined, my leisure time is much more limited than when I was Town Majoring.

†Phyllis Nield, later to become his wife.
‡John Ronald Hardman, Pattie & Tom's son.

We came down here two days ago for a week's rest, having had five weeks up in the line, and we are having quite a good time. I have not seen Frank Hayes since he came back. Last night I received your letter of June 7th in which you state that he called round to see you. I saw him the day before he left here & at that time I was expecting to come on the same boat, so he would quite expect me being at home whilst he was; however it was not to be so I have still got the full ten days to look forward to. No doubt I shall arrive at Arnwood in three weeks time, but not before then, so do not let the thoughts of my appearing in the early hours of the morning disturb your sleep at all.

The Colonel informed me last night that he had again sent my name forward for a second pip so I hope it will come along before my leave, as I do not want to come home again as a 2/Lt.

I was awfully sorry to hear that Alan Preston had been killed; you might give Mr & Mrs Preston my deepest sympathy, if I have time I'll write.

From all accounts our Eastern kit which we had sent from Egypt has been sunk. I had not much of value in mine, but there were some photographs which cannot be replaced, taken when I was with Joe Chatterton in Cairo. I very nearly put the shawls etc in, so I tap myself on the back that I thought twice. I'm in the pink of condition & hope that you are the same.

July 2 1917

I have got another surprise for you; for the next three weeks address my letters to

3rd Corps School
B.E.F.

I have come down here for one month so I shall not be home so early as I thought. In fact if I had not come down here I should have come home this weekend. Do not be disappointed, as I shall take my leave as soon as this Course is over, so it is only postponed for a week or two and in the meantime I'm having quite an interesting time well back away from the line. In fact I'm beginning to think there is a Fairy Godmother or some other such wonderful being of the olden days hovering over me since I've been in France. No matter which way I turn, I seem to land on my jolly old feet every time, it's really most remarkable.

How are you getting along? Had your summer holidays yet, or are you taking them in short weekends at Milner Avenue? The last time I wrote to you was from our rest billets and a couple of days afterwards we moved up into the line. I was there for two days then left to come up here, and by Jove I was mighty pleased. Owing to recent rains the trenches were in a filthy condition, in fact more like canals, and it is simply wretched living in the trenches under those conditions. No more for the present, so Au Revoir.

Your Son
Jack

July 5 1917

Just a few lines to let you know that I'm in the pink & having quite a good time.

Yesterday I spent in Amiens, the very first Town I have been in since coming to France, so you can understand how it was appreciated. For a start I visited the toilet salon & had a top-hole shave & shampoo; at the same time I had my moustache taken off which quite disguised me (I don't think) and we finished up with a tip-top dinner & landed back here at 1 o'clock A.M.

By the way, do you mind sending me out another watch the same as the last one which unfortunately I have broken, & have now been without one for three weeks & it's awfully boring having to ask what time it is when one wakens up in the morning, especially if one happens to waken up rather early & wakens his neighbour to ask him the time, to discover it is only about 5 o'clock. In fact one is liable to be severely told off (I might say it does not very often happen to me, but it might) so I will take the necessary precautions by getting one of my own.

I have just come off the Range and incidentally I shot rather well (revolver shooting). I will now put the lid on as I have no more news, so Au Revoir. Hoping you are both in the best of health.

I remain
Your Son
Jack

July 8 1917
France

Being Sunday I will write you the usual Sunday epistle although it will be rather short owing to lack of news.

Yesterday I received Father's letter of June 26th in which he said it was a long time since you had heard from me, well perhaps so, but you must understand that when in the Trenches one has not the time for writing as frequently as one would like.

I also received the parcel of biscuits & parkin which was top-hole. This last two days the weather has been glorious. I hope you are having the same. No more for the present, so Au Revoir

Your Son
Jack

France
July 17 1917

Yesterday I received your letter of the 8th written on the back of envelopes for which you apologised; if it had been written on fine Vellum at 5/- a square inch I would not have noticed any difference.

I must tell you that last Sunday I had a ripping day. My usual sparring partner & self cleared off to Amiens for the day, and we had not been in the place ten minutes when we bumped into Baty, Baker & Douglas Stephenson who had just arrived on a day's leave. Well need I say more? We spent the whole day together until 8 o'clock PM when I saw then off on the train & two hours later we rejoined our bus & left for home ourselves. Yesterday the watch arrived; it is just the thing & I thank you very much.

I have acknowledged in a previous letter the arrival of the scotch cake etc. The scotch cake & parkin are a great success & they came in awfully handy after the Mess was closed; about six of us retired to our tent & had supper.

Did Father have much to say to the fellow Marshall whom he met in M/c? If so you might say what impression father has of him. Isn't the weather tip-top now? Baty informed me that he had received a parcel from you.

France
July 23rd 1917

I received your letter of July 16th two days ago. I spent the weekend in Amiens & had quite a decent time, but all the same, to my mind there is no place like M/c or Stockport, and with a bit of luck I shall be there very shortly now.

I hear that Baker has gone & in the ordinary way of things I was due about 10 days before him, but whilst I have been here two of them have gone from D Coy, so it sounds pretty hopeful for me after my course is over which is in 7 days, so cheer up. If I come in August I shall spend most of my time at the Villa in Blackpool. I did my best to write a letter of consolation to Mrs Preston a week ago, but have not yet posted it. You know it is rather a ticklish problem to a brainless joker to concoct such a letter; however after serious consideration I have at last decided to post it. It will at any rate translate my feelings however clumsily worded it may be.

You will be pleased to hear that one of our Officers has been awarded the *M.C.* for a very daring & well carried-out raid. Remember me to everybody. Best love to yourselves

I remain
Your Son
Jack

France
July 29 1917

I received your letter of July 22nd written on your birthday, if it not too late ''Very Many Happy Returns''. Today is Sunday, the last Sunday I shall spend here as I return to the Battalion in three days, so instead of going to Amiens I am endeavouring to finish off all my correspondence.

Tomorrow & the day after we are finishing up the Course with Sports. I have entered for one or two races just for the sport of the thing as I'm rather too fat to hope of winning any of them. Of course being weighty has its advantages: I'm picked for the Tug of War team.

From the papers I see that the old Bosch has been paying some more Flying Visits to London.

Whilst I'm writing this there is rather a severe thunderstorm in progress. I don't know whether you've had much thunder this summer, but over here there has been quite a lot. I hope to be home sometime next month so you had better tell Pat to have a spare bed aired in her Seaside Residence. For the present Au Revoir.

August 3 1917

I'm now back with the Battalion who are at present well away from the firing line, training pretty hard. Since I rejoined the weather has been atrocious, pouring down the whole day. I expect to be home about the 20th. I should really have been coming today but I have had it done on me, so to speak. I hope you are quite well, personally I'm in the pink.

FRANCE SECOND TRIP

30/8/17
British Officers Club

My Dear Mother & Father,

At last I have landed in France & hope to rejoin the Batt_ tomorrow. Last night I spent in London & had quite a good time with Mr Nield[†] & Mr Granger who very kindly stood me a meal & afterwards the Theatre. It was awfully funny, I was walking round the City feeling somewhat lonely & fed up when whom should I bump into but Mr Granger; he laughed like blazes. I knew he was there but I did not know where he was staying, so wasn't it a stroke of luck? I will write again when I rejoin the Batt so goodbye

Best Love
Jack

Sept 1 1917

My Dear Mother & Father,

Since leaving home I've had quite a number of experiences. In the first place, when the train got to Miller's Dale quite a number of people got in, amongst them an old lady who planted herself next to me in the Dining Saloon & much to my annoyance would insist on carrying on a conversation with me. Of course I had to be polite & answer her briefly although I was endeavouring to digest the contents of a cheap novel which I bought on the station. However the dear old thing came in quite useful as when we arrived in London I could not get a taxi for love or money & she would insist on me getting into her car & driving me to the station. We had quite an affectionate parting & having given me her card, she made me promise to write & say if I had arrived safely or not.

I told you that I had spent the night in London with Mr Granger & Mr Nield & now I'm back with the Battalion. I have now got two surprises for you; the first is that I believe my name has appeared in the Gazette as a full Lieutenant (if you can get the Times of 29th & 30th & send it to me as I believe it appeared on one of those dates).

Now for the second surprise: the C.O. was so annoyed at my getting an extension that he ordered my arrest as soon as I got back without ever consulting me on whose Authority I got the extension. It is one of the biggest jokes in the Battalion as he will have such a shock at

[†]Mr Nield - later to become his father-in-law.

our first interview when I show him the War Office Telegram. It is not what one would call a very good reception on one's return from leave, is it? I cannot tell you where we are, but most probably Baker will be able to; have you seen him yet?

I hope you are having good weather at St Anne's. If you will be advised by me you will stay there at least a month as it is awfully bracing & that is what both of you want, something to buck you up. All for the present.

I remain
With Best Love
Jack

September 8 1917

My Dear Mother & Father,

Just a few lines from my dirty old dug-out. Yes, I am once again in the thick of it, leave being a thing of the past for me for several months yet. At the present moment I have rather a responsible position being in command of the Coy.

Thorpe is now at home & will most probably have called round before this reaches you. Capt Higham has left the Battalion & is now 2nd-in-Command of the 6th Lancashire Fusiliers, the same Batt_ as Lindley Henshaw & Nip Heydon.

My arrest was an absolute washout. Do you remember me telling you about my batman? Well you may be surprised to hear that I sacked him the second day I arrived back. Have you seen Baker yet? & is he as cheerful as ever? I'm so pleased you had a good time at St Anne's, but what on Earth made you decide to return so soon passes my comprehension. In fact a month would not be too long for you, & there is no Earthly reason why you should not have a month's holiday somewhere. You might send me the Stockport Weekly Papers will you, & carry on with the parcels as we have now left the training camp that I told you of & therefore have not the same elaborate Mess.

September 12 1917

Just a few lines from the trenches to say that I'm in the pink & feeling very fit just having partaken of some of the ripping parkin which I received this afternoon.

Father's letter amused us terribly talking about a Court Martial as there were no grounds whatever for a C.M. As soon as I pulled the little bit of paper which I had in my pocket from the W.O. they were rather sorry that they had been so hasty in my drastic treatment; however all that is now a thing of the past.

Whilst in the line I'm in command of the Coy which is rather a responsibility, having 200 men & 2 Officers in the Coy; however it is quite good practice for the day when I shall have reached the position of Captain or perhaps higher, one never knows.

You will no doubt hear that Joe Chatterton has been wounded. Poor old Joe, he was just as cheery as ever although he had one leg broken in three places. Still he has finished with fighting. Sam Baker was out when you called. I had a letter from him & he said you had not seen him.

Now, whatever you do you must not worry, because most wounds nowadays are soft ones & I don't think that I shall even get one of those.

Best Love

Jack

PS As they are always telling me, I was not born to be shot while there is enough rope in the World to hang me with, so cheery ho.

October 13 1917

A few lines to inform you that I'm still jogging along, but this weather does feed me up; however it will not be long I hope before this d- War is over.

I heard from Joe yesterday, the old bird is quite cheerful, although he said another 2 inches had to be taken off his foot. I've also heard that Baker is now out of the Army, lucky old thing. Did I tell you that he wrote me the day after he had been to Arnwood & from the tone of his letter you had quite a good time together.

The other day I received another parcel from you containing cake etc, for which I thank you, but up to writing I have not received my cigs from Father. I have just received your letter dated the 8th, rather good coming in 4 days, isn't it? No more for the present so Au Revoir

---

October 17 1917

Just a few lines whilst I have the opportunity to tell you that I'm in the pink of condition & sincerely hope that you are the same. As you know we are at present out of the line in a Village living in Billets. It is quite nice except for the numerous parades we have, & as you know I get awfully fed up with parades; however tomorrow morning I am going away for four days on a Gas Course, so that will be somewhat of a rest.

I have received your parcel of parkin & biscuits for which I thank you, also the parcel of cigarettes from Father. These could not have come at a more opportune time as I had been without cigs for two days owing to the fact that where we now are it is rather difficult to get English cigs.

The weather has reformed again & the last two days have been glorious. Capt Higham expects to be coming home on leave in about a week's time & if possible he will arrange to see Father, but ten days is not very long so I have told him that although Father would like to see him very much, he must not trouble if he has not the time. I hope you are both well as this letter leaves me.

E.F.C. Officers Rest House & Mess
Oct 20 1917

Having just partaken of some of the parkin which arrived three days ago I'm feeling very pleased with life. By this time you will be quite used to my flitting about so it will not surprise you very much when I tell you that I'm not with the Batt_ at present. I'm down here for a few days learning all there is to know about Gas and also anti-gas measures. I shall be quite clever if this War lasts long enough. The above address is where we Mess whilst here, but do not send my letters here as I shall be back with the Batt_ before this reaches you.

Do you know that Baker is out of the Army, isn't he lucky? At the present time the weather is quite good although a little bit cold at night. By the way, I've sent some more surplus kit home. When it arrives will you look if my British Warm (overcoat) is in; I can't find it here in my kit so I presume that my Orderly has sent it home in a mistake. Let me know immediately because he is coming on leave shortly; he lives in the neighbourhood of Lostock St., so he can meet Father on Rent Day & bring back my coat. Do not get excited & think that your dear Jack is without a coat because he is not, having got the Burberry with fleecy lining which he bought when on leave, & once I'm in that I'm as warm as toast, but I should like my coat for slipping on occasionally.

---

3 November 1917

I have had several letters from you since I wrote but owing to having been locked up in a concrete dug-out for six days I have not had the opportunity. In this place there are ten of us. It is only 3ft 6 high & about 4ft square. In the daytime we dare not show our nose outside &

as soon as it is dark enough we are all working at the different Posts, our working hours being from 5.30 pm to 6 am when we creep back into our warrens just as dawn is breaking & I can tell you, by this time I'm about ready for sleep & don't as a rule wake up much before dusk when I'm busy again. This is my sixth day of this life; in two days time we go out of the line for a rest so I will then write you a longer letter.

I'm so sorry to hear of your indisposition & hope you are now better. I rather fancy the cause of it is that you have been worrying about me, it is very silly of you because it does no good whatever. Best love to both of you. Will write again in a few days.

---

11 November 1917

Have just received your letter of 7th for which I thank you. By the time you receive this father will have seen my Batman up at the buildings. It is Sunday today so probably he will see him tomorrow. At the present time we are out of the trench I'm pleased to say, as the Sector we are at present on is quite the worst we have struck, not so much for the actual fighting but the conditions of the place. Where I lived was a concrete pill-box about 3ft 6 high & 5ft square. In the daytime I could not put my nose outside as the old Bosche, whenever he saw the least sign of its occupation, would paste it with shells, so the whole day long we were cut off from the World so to speak & got our rations & water up to us under cover of darkness.

I'm all right for winter underclothing. By the way, Pa, do you mind paying into Cox & Co £10 for me? The other day I had an intimation from them that my account was overdrawn & would I please remit. Well of course it does not matter very much as it will be quite all right when I have this month's allowances paid in, but the Paymaster is often late & I would not like to have any cheques returned, so you might do this for me will you?

I'm afraid to disappoint you, but I shall not be home for Xmas; at the earliest it will be the end of January '18 unless the War is over before then "I don't think".

There is not much to write about except that I had a taste of civilisation for two days. After we had had four days in the front line we came down into the Support line & there the C.O. gave permission to Capt Nidd & myself to go down & have a good clean up. We went to ------- on the coast, stayed at the Hotel -------- for a couple of days & it was really a wonderful transformation, all in about six hours from No-Man's-Land to a first class Hotel & have a decent dinner. No more for the present.

Nov 21st 1917

My Dear Father,

I have just received you letter of the 16th inst. We have just completed a five days march, each night staying at different farmhouses, quite interesting though somewhat tiring to the feet, but I can't grumble as my poor old feet came up to scratch & finished feeling none the worse than when I started.

Where we now are is quite a cosy little place & we are here for at least four days. I note that you have seen my Orderly & given him the coat etc. What do you think of him rather an ancient creature isn't he ? I'm afraid when he comes back he will have rather a surprise as the one I have now as a substitute whilst he's been away suits me so well that I think I shall stick to him & give the old chap the order of the boot.

I hope you have a good time on the anniversary of Pat's Wedding. I did not realise it was so near until I received your letter & I'm afraid it is rather late now to send them a card. Thanks very much for putting my a/c at Cox's square, you are a dear old sport.

I had a little present from P_ last night in the shape of a parcel of gramophone records, quite the latest out, it's awfully good of her isn't it? By the way do you mind sending me out two pairs of pants. I have two pairs but I find it rather difficult with regards to the washing, also two suits of pyjamas. I haven't any at all, both my last two pairs I wore until they were in shreds.

During the march I was attached to Capt Nidd's Company as he was rather short of Officers, but am going back to D Coy tomorrow. Although Nidd is a topping chap I would much rather be in old D Coy. It is about bed time now so I will ring off.

Nov 24 1917

My Dear Mother,

Have just received your letter of 18th & am now answering it in quite a cosy little place. We arrived here three days ago & have fairly struck oil. The old dame at my billet is quite a dear old creature. On my bed (feather) I have white sheets & as many blankets as I require.

Our Mess is in the "Estaminet" (Village Pub). We have quite a dinky little room & a warm fire so taking things all round we are not doing too badly. My Orderly is two or three days overdue, seems to have lost himself somewhere on this side of the Channel.

Did I tell you P_ has sent me some lovely records for the gramophone, every week Dick's girl sends me the Tatler & I have received all your parcels, so things are not as bad as you seem to imagine. Unfortunately your last parcel had a rough passage, the glass jar was broken so the lemon cheese escaped. For Xmas you can't do better than what you did last year.

By today's mail I also had another letter from Beatrice. You will be surprised to hear that we have another fresh C.O. Our late one has had an operation in England which unfortunately will keep him there for some time. Our Company Sgt-Major is coming home on leave in three days; I would like Father to meet him, he is a regular "old stiff" so I will tell him to meet Father at the buildings as he lives down there somewhere.

I met Leslie Haws last night, he is quite fit. I heard from Baker the other day. He is now studying hard for his exams. Two of my old Platoon received the Military Medal for good work the last time we were in the line; of course now I'm 2nd-in-Command I do not have a Platoon although I still have a soft spot in my heart for the old Platoon.

PS. Will you ask Father to send out 2,000 Woodbines, a little Xmas gift for the old Platoon. I'll square up with him.

Nov 29th 1917

We have now finished our long trek & are once again holding the Line. At least so we are told but it is such a quiet front to what we have recently experienced that it is hard to imagine that we are anywhere near the Frontline.

I'm sending home three watches which I want repairing; have tried all over France, but owing to shortage of labour cannot get them repaired here. Two are mine, but the one with the metal lid over the face is one of the Subs in the Company, so let me know the price of each individual watch; by the way, if any of them want much doing don't bother as it will cost as much as a new watch, but I think they only want slight repairs such as cleaning etc. There is no great hurry as I still have one which Baker left me.

My Orderly has not arrived back yet; we can't make out where he has got to because he was seen in France on his way back by several men who were returning at the same time. Today the Padre had lunch with me & he told me that Baty was coming back to us, so I don't think he will bother with the Flying Corps now. Franklin, the fellow whom Father met when Baty was on leave, has now left us; you know his Mother was a widow & his two brothers have been killed in the War, so the Battalion applied for him to be put on a soft job & he has got something on the L of C. He was awfully sick at leaving the Batt_ but I think it is a good thing considering the circumstances, don't you?

I saw Corporal Lockett the other day & he told me that he had met an *old gentleman* in M/c who asked after me; of course I knew at once who it was from the description. How is Joe Chatterton? No-one in the Battalion has heard from him for about two months & we are awfully anxious. Will write again at the first opportunity. Hoping you are both jolly well & not becoming too pessimistic as to the duration of the War, because we are fairly humping the old Bosche. I remain In the pink of condition.

Dec 3 1917

My Dear Mother,

I have just received your letter of Nov 28th. Pleased to see that you are once again in your old cheerful mood. Although we are now back in the trenches I'm enjoying the best of health. My Orderly arrived back two days ago with the coat etc. He informed me that the next time he is over, you asked him over to Stockport & that he had to remind me about writing every so often. I've decided he is too old for this job & my present Orderly is quite a young lad.

I'm awfully pleased that you had a good time at Mrs Smith's, surely she never thought that B & I were serious. Where on Earth did you pick up the knitted sleeping cap which you sent along? It is the very thing I can tell you for this job especially as this morning we had the first signs of frost.

The reason I have not a Platoon at present is that I am 2nd-in-Command of the Coy. Baty is awfully lucky if he gets home in January again; I'm afraid it will be after that 'ere my turn comes round again. Where we now are is quite the quietest sector of the Line we have been in, so you need not worry.†

Dec 11 1917

You will be pleased to hear that at the present moment I am in quite the most homelike billet it has been my luck to strike in France. After having had 12 days in the trenches we came down here for six days training & rest, then we have another spell of six days in the trenches and then 12 days out‡, which should carry us over Xmas & New Year's Day.

The parcel of pyjamas & pants have arrived. Last night I got in bed decked in my new pyjamas, & by gad what a treat! It was the very first time I had had pyjamas on since my leave.

The morning after we arrived here three of us were sitting in the billet before a blazing fire when your parcel arrived, so I opened it (''toute suite'' as they say in French) – imagine our

†Wilson reports: We were now at the seaside and there was the usual crop of mad holiday projects. One of these was to experiment with a new gas to be projected onto the Bosche front trench across the river. Then Lt. Morten was to pilot a boat over, hop into the said trench and return in possession of a "gassee" from whom the results would be studied. Morten went down the line with a sturdy crew of AB's from D Coy to practise rowing, but luckily that was as far as the scheme progressed. Then we had out sea serpent.......

‡The official system was 4 days in the front line, 4 days in support, 4 days in the line, 4 days in Brigade reserve. After 32 days of this the Brigade went out for 16 days in Division reserve. They were near Nieuport Bains on the River Yser. It was the westernmost end of the western front.

faces when we saw 15 dinky little pieces of paper with a mince pie in each one. We called Mademoiselle, ordered a bottle of bock, and had an eleven o'clock lunch consisting of a couple of each. They were simply delicious, you quite excelled yourself.

By the way, the cake which was in the parcel is quite an improvement on the ones you have recently sent, it is not so dry.

Dec 20th 1917

My Dear Mother & Father,

It is very near to Xmas Day now & I sincerely hope that you will have a topping time. There is every prospect of it being quite a good time out here. In two days we go out of the trenches for 12 days rest which will carry us over Xmas & New Year, & apart from anything else we shall be billeted in ---------- which is quite a large & civilised town.

I don't know whether I told you, but Major Hirst is back with us, and as in the old days he's been most energetic providing entertainments & grub etc for the men on the famous Day. He has also written a play which is being performed before the General on or about the 27th – much to my annoyance he has me down for a part. Did my best to cry off, as you know I do not relish making a fool of myself in public, however he would not take a negative reply, so I have had quite a busy time learning my part.

I received your parcels & papers about a week ago & the greater part of the former are now consumed. The turkey was fine – by the way we had it whilst in the trenches; rather high living for the trenches, what! At the present time the weather is topping, quite a keen frost; every morning we turn out of bed to have a trip round the trenches & find everything enveloped in snow & there is a lovely crispness about the air which makes you feel full of vim. No doubt you will be pulling a long face saying to dear old Father "How cold the poor boy must be"; well, do you know, I brought up with me nothing but my British Warm in the way of warm clothing; this I wear at night & wrap my feet up in sand-bags & I'm as warm as toast, in fact as you know I have got some thick winter undervests in my valise & I have not yet started to wear them. I'm becoming quite a hardened old veteran, what do you say, although I'm not looking forward to the wet weather, but so long as it is dry it's tres bon.

A MERRY XMAS
&
A HAPPY NEW YEAR
YOUR SON
Jack

Dec 31st 1917

Just a few lines to wish you a Very Happy New Year & I sincerely hope that you had a jolly good Xmas. The Xmas out here was a far greater success than any of us anticipated; of course we were awfully fortunate in being out of the Line. We gave the men a topping time, they had the best Xmas dinner which they have yet had in the Army. It consisted of turkey, pork, vegs, plum pudding & rum sauce, washed down with beer. The Officers & Sergeants waited on & they thoroughly enjoyed it. This was at midday & our little do came off at night.

Then two days afterwards our little Play was performed & it was a howling success, in fact we were asked to give it again tonight, but owing to several working parties which we have had to provide it has been cancelled, much to my relief incidentally.

Higham is now back again with us. The other day he, myself & another Subaltern in the Coy went shopping to --------. We had a great time; it was really most amusing what with our Pigeon French & their Pigeon English. We bought three topping fur collars for our coats; apart from the warmth we derive from them we look awful knuts. Must close now so Au Revoir.

Jan 1st 1918

A few lines as there is nothing like beginning the New Year well is there?

Last night we had quite a good time & we waited up to see the New Year in. My usual good luck attended me; the old Bosche thought he would be funny so came over in his aeroplanes bombing us, and would you believe it, he dropped one right on my cosy billet, absolutely wrecked the house, wounded the occupant & incidentally scattered by belongings all over the place.

I suppose you are now wondering how it is I'm not scattered in little bits, well I'll tell you. Earlier on we had orders for one Officer and 80 men to proceed up the Line for working from 4pm till 11pm. I was detailed much to my disgust & cursed my bad luck for having to go up the Line on New Year's Eve. Having finished our work we came back, so off I trotted to the Mess (about 11.30pm) & found all the Officers having a sing-song & waiting for the New Year. As soon as I opened the door everybody shrieked with laughter, of course I wondered what was wrong, then was informed that I had no home, & one of the Officers put me up for the night in his billet.

I was awfully anxious to see my late home & went to have a look at it & imagine my surprise when I saw the wreckage of my bed with all my kit balancing on one of the cross beams which had remained in position. So this morning my servant had quite a busy time climbing up & throwing my things down to a fellow who was holding a blanket in the street catching them; of course it is a pretty risky business climbing to the second floor of a house which has been badly bent because you never know when the remainder is going to fall.

It's rather a scream & I thank my lucky stars that I was detailed for the working party or I should most certainly have been in the house when the catastrophe happened. The whole thing has been a huge joke amongst us, especially when I arrived home at midnight to find myself homeless, but looking at it from the other side it's a d_____ shame as the occupants, a man, his wife & two kiddies are now without a home & most of their hard-earned savings gone; ah well "It's the War" & I suppose the same thing will happen again & again until the whole thing shoots over.

If you can't make out all these disjointed sentences please excuse as Baty & the Padre are arguing like two old women. The best of luck to both of you.

In the opening days of the New Year they returned to the Brickstacks sector south of the Canal. It was very muddy and wet.

"This amphibious warfare was extremely unpleasant and it further delayed work on the new defensive positions. Capt. Jimmy Baker and Lt Jack Morten, whilst on a midnight prowl in No Man's Land, almost met with disaster, and the performance came to an undignified close after they had extricated one another from deep muddy water to make their way back to dock minus gum boots." – S.J. Wilson, The Seventh Manchesters.

Feb 2 1918

My Dear Mother,

Have received your letter of Jan 27th. Yes, I received the topping parcel of mince pies & also the two watches. As you say, living on half a pound of meat a week will not fatten anybody; however it will be quite worth it when all is over & we can look upon the Hun as defeated. It rather feeds me up to hear about the people in M/c making a fuss at being rationed, because one half of them did not realise there was a War on until then, & so, as soon as the War interferes with their comfort they squeal like so many babies & cry for peace.

We are not in the trenches & don't expect we will be for another six weeks as we're going back for training & at the end of that time my leave should be about due.

I've just had some patterns sent out from a London tailor so that I shall be able to have a decent pair of breeches to come home in. Thorpe is now back in the Coy. According to the newspaper accounts London has had another Air Raid. Father might write to Hupfeld & ask him what he thinks about our raids over Mannheim. I hope it keeps fine for Hupfeld's relations; I often wonder how much of the celluloid factory is still standing. I had quite an amusing letter from Mr Brooks; you might tell him that it was the means of four jaded officers (just out of the line) taking an interest in life once more. There is not much to write about so will close.

Feb 12 1918

Just a few lines to say that I'm in the pink except voiceless, can't even carry on a conversation; however I suppose a mere flash in the pan, it will most probably be better in a day or two. The reason you've had so few letters from me is because for the last two weeks I've been in Command of the Company & you know what that means, so I crave your forgiveness. I came down here yesterday for five weeks on a Company Commander's Course so you can see I've struck oil. It is an ideal spot just near Boulogne. We've every imaginable sport including a topping golf course. Our Mess is in a lovely old Chateau with every modern comfort. A company of the W.A.A.C.'s are on the Mess staff & last but not least we've one of the finest bands in France which plays us on parade every morning & plays in the Mess two or three nights a week. For the next four weeks will you address my letters to

L-
Regt
1st Army Inf. Course
B.E.F.
Bon Soir, hoping you are in the best of health.

With Love
Jack

Feb 17 1918

I have just received your letter of the 8th, for which many thanks. There is very little to write about but I thought you would like a line to say that I'm in tip-top health except for my voice which has entirely disappeared & I cannot always voice my opinions which is rather annoying (to me) sometimes. I saw the M.O. yesterday & he said probably it would be a week before it returned. The funniest thing is when we are on parade & have to number; all I can do is to make a great effort & a little squeak issues forth. The Instructor, who is perhaps 100 yds away hears nothing & gets quite excited because no.__ is asleep. Then amidst a peal of laughter it is explained to him that no.__ has no voice.

Yesterday being Saturday I went to Boulogne & had a topping bath. Oh well, my news is now finished so will close.

I remain
Your Son
Jack

Feb 23 1918

A few lines from France telling you that the Warrior is still O.K., yes, and as long as he stops here he will be; really you've no idea what a delightful spot this place is; I will try and describe it and leave the rest to your imagination (I've no doubt that Father will with ease be able to supply the necessary imagination).

Here we are living in an ancient abbey with beautiful grounds in which are tennis courts, golf links, football & hockey grounds including a Lake all in the Park, and outside the grounds on the one hand we've the sea with all its exhilarating breezes, and on the other a huge pine forest where we occasionally drop across a wild boar. We have two half holidays & the whole of Sunday off every week, so you see we are not overworked. So far I've done better than on my previous courses but seeing that I've still got another two weeks I must not start boasting (touch wood).

By the way Father, I've an idea that you once bought me some War Bonds but I never hear of any dividend, will you please let me know how many I've actually got. I'm now suggesting something which will no doubt be rather a surprise to you; would it be quite agreeable to you if I transferred to the Regular Army & thus pursued a professional career, because I don't really see very great prospects in a commercial one? Well, I will now close, hoping to hear from you soon.

I remain
Your Son
Jack

PS. When you answer the above question do not let any sickly sentiment guide your thoughts. What I mean to say is that say perhaps I went to a Foreign Station, as you know you would only see me occasionally, but I'm sure you would prefer that to seeing me every day & only one of the miserable pen-pushers of the City earning perhaps £3 a week.

March 11 1918

My Dear Mother & Father,

A few hurried lines to let you know that I'm having a topping time; the weather is so absolutely gorgeous that it would be a crime to stay inside writing a long letter.

Yesterday (Sunday) I had a fine game of La Crosse; we beat a colonial team. In the evening attended church service, however I must not take all the credit for this, it was really my servant who suggested to me in a very respectful way that seeing that I had not attended a service since coming on the course "I might like to go", so I went & enjoyed the Service very much. It was Motherly Sunday so the Padre informed us (some special day which the C. of E. recognise) & at the end of the service we had a short prayer for you dear old things at home. In my own mind I'm rather undecided whether to go over to the C. of E. or not.

I must tell you this, the last mail brought me two large photos of P_, they are simply charming. My voice is returning very slowly. Well must close now with tons of love.

I remain
Yours
Jack

E.F.C.
Officers' Rest House &
Mess
March 18 1918

My Dear Mother & Father,

My life of ease is now at an end as tomorrow I rejoin the Battalion, but I'm living in hopes that my leave will come round very soon. As soon as I get back I shall enquire & will let you know when to expect me. Baty has got his Captaincy so I shall receive mine when the next vacancy occurs (whenever that is). You see, although Baty & I were gazetted on the same day, he is my senior because his name appears on the Army List before mine. I'm off now to the Picture Palace so bon soir. Hoping you are in the best of health.

I remain
Yours with Love
Jack

J.C.Morten was wounded on March 27th 1918 near Ablainzevelle on the western edge of Havrincourt Wood.

..................."The entrance was cleared, steps constructed again, and work carried on as usual. "D" Company lost its commander again, for Lieut. Morten was hit, and this left Lieut. Gresty in charge.[e.] *S.J. Wilson, The Seventh Manchesters.*

April 5th – Stockport Advertiser: Lieut. J Morten, M/c Regt, son of Mr & Mrs C.S. Morten of Beech Road, Stockport, has been wounded and is in hospital.

ENGLAND

Dear Mother & Father,

I arrived here quite in order yesterday & it is quite a bon place, especially in comparison to the place where I existed last week. Did you enjoy the theatre last night? You will find my address on the other side. Kind regards to Tom & Pat.

June 4 1918

My Dear Father,

Thank you very much for the money received this morning. Ever since I arrived back I have been awfully busy, first of all preparing the lecture which I delivered with great eclat this morning, so now that is off my chest I am preparing for tomorrow's Exam. Had quite a pleasant journey on Sunday although I felt very cheap towards the end of Monday. You will find enclosed cheque for £10, five of which is my first instalment of the little loan I floated. I trust that Mother is quite well, give her my love & don't forget the instructions as to the distribution of my photos when they arrive. Well I will now ring off, hoping that you are in the pink.

I remain
Your Son
Jack

Post Card
June 9 1918

A few lines to let you know I am in the pink but feeling horribly fed up, this being the first weekend I have been away from home since arriving in Blighty. I am now sharing a tent with an old Pal from D Coy who reported here whilst I was away, so that improves things a little. Hoping you are quite fit.

June 16 1918

A few lines to say that I'm in the pink & have just missed going out again. The War Office appear to have my name off by heart. Yesterday we sent a draft away including six Officers & the War Office actually detailed me; the only thing which kept me back was my certificate from the R.A.F. so it was not such a rash thing on my part when I applied to the R.A.F. as you first imagined, was it? There was one Officer, a Captain who has been here a much shorter time than I have; in fact it was three weeks after my wound that he was hit & he had to go last night.

At the present moment it is raining furiously which does not at all cheer one so fed up as the humble writer. By the way Father, will you send me £5 per return if poss; I have driven it rather late & at the present moment do not posses 5/- in cash. I will send you on a cheque as soon as it arrives. I think I will now get to my bed as I have to be up tomorrow at 5.30 AM.

June 24 1918

I suppose Phyll will have told you that I was down with the 'Flu, well I am now past the milk stage & am on ordinary diet; of course you will observe by the writing that I am still in bed. Awfully strange, isn't it, 26 Officers & 400 men, quite an epidemic.

On Thursday Thorpe came into my tent temporarily, of course caught the 'flu from me I suppose, so we are now still in the same tent. I received the registered letter this morning, for which thanks very much. I cannot just place my hands on my cheque book & if I get up & start moving around most probably my head will come on again, so you don't mind waiting a day or so, do you? Hoping you're quite fit.
(Followed by telegram dated 26.6.18) Much better thanks Jack.

Post Card
Dear Mother, June 26 1918

Am quite well, went out today for 1st time. What was the idea of the telegram this morning? I haven't yet solved the idea. Hope Father is quite fit in spite of this spell of cold weather.

Cheery ho
Jack

June 28 1918

Here we are again, this time fully recovered & my own self once more. Am still anxiously awaiting orders from the R.A.F. which are taking rather longer than I expected. I am herewith enclosing £10, £5 is for the money you sent me the other day & the other £5 is my 2nd instalment of the famous loan with Father. By the way, have my photographs arrived yet? It is quite time they did. The other day I heard from Baker who informed me that Higham was at home for six months, have you seen anything of him yet? In closing I should like to remind you that your letters are very few & very short & that although I'm at Scarboro the local news of Davenport & the people there still interest me. Hoping you're in the best of health.

Burniston
Scarborough
July 2 1918

Having just finished a tip-top meal I will drop you a few lines before going out on duty. Phyll will no doubt have been round & told you about my new job; if only I can stay here until the R.A.F. send for me it will be tip top. My landlady made a rhubarb pie today & served it up with cream (doesn't that make your mouth water). If it was not for all the walking about I have to do I should get too fat if here for long. The weather at present is simply glorious. Last night we had a drop of rain but nothing worth speaking about. Colin Thorpe is going in for the R.A.F. & is at present in London undergoing his medical examination. I have not heard from you now for over a week & I know you're not so awfully busy that you have not the time; you're both getting very lazy in your old age is the conclusion I've come to, so consider yourselves told off. In future address my letters to

Lt_
Boundary House
Cloughton
Nr Scarboro

will you, as this is my new residence. It is awfully quiet. I don't see anybody except when I'm visiting my different Posts, so my spare time is taken up by listening to my landlady telling me all the Village scandal, quite a rest cure. Well good bye, hoping you are in the best of health.

July 9 1918

So sorry you could not come, it's such a pity when there was such an opportunity for all living together. However if you decide when Phyll is better, all you have to do is to send a telegram & everything will be ready at this end for you, of course the longer you drive it, the less likelihood there is of me still being here, but as soon as I move I'll send you a telegram, then you will know. I have just sent Phyll some flowers grown by the local Village Grocer who looks upon me as being a great person as I'm the Military Representative. I very nearly bought a motor cycle the other day, but could not come to terms about the price I'm sorry to say, as it would be awfully useful to me on this job. Isn't the weather glorious? Last night we had a bit of a thunderstorm which lasted for about half an hour; no damage except that a sheep in the field next to my house was struck by lightning. Well must away now.

July 11 1918

I have just received your letter & am very pleased you are coming on Monday. Could you not have managed this weekend though? At present I've no idea how long my sojourn here will be, but the sooner you come the better. Thorpe came to see me the other day & he is very fed up with his interview with the R.A.F. After being examined they said that he was not fit in any capacity for the R.A.F., rather bad luck isn't it? I ordered some fresh butter for you, then thinking you would be here this week, told them to hold it over. No more for the present. Come as soon as you can, a wire is quite sufficient.

July 23 1918

So pleased to hear you arrived home safely & in good time & hope you feel better for the change. It was a ripping week, wasn't it? By the way, what was your bill at Cockerill's? Do you know, that day we had the trap from 2 pm until 8.15 pm they only charged me 4/-, wasn't it awfully cheap? I hope the business which took Father home turned out successfully. It seems awfully quiet here now having all my meals by myself after the noise of last week. I'm now off to Hayburn Wyke so good bye.

July 28 1918

No doubt you will be surprised to hear that I have moved from Boundary House & am now living at Hayburn Wyke. I had the shock of my life on Friday when an Officer turned up at

Boundary House to inform me that he had come to take over my job & that I had to take over the Hayburn Wyke Detachment.

On Friday afternoon I wrote a very strong letter to the Adj asking him the reason, pointing out that I had never received any complaints from H.Q's as to any non-compliance of orders or laxity on my part whilst being in command here. I also pointed out that during all my Army Career I had never been treated with such an indignity. In reply the Adj wrote me an awfully decent letter full of apologies & said it was an error, but the C.O. directed that I must move my H.Q's to Hayburn Wyke & that the Officer at Boundary House would be under me. So far so good, but not quite to my liking, so on Saturday morning I went down to the Battalion & told him that I could not carry out my duties unless I had the assistance of another Officer, & without any demur he said he would send another Lieut out also. So you see, after all I have not done so badly, having got two more Officers on my strength; I shall have a much easier time, but all the same I would have preferred to stay at Boundary House & done the extra work myself. However, I'm awfully pleased I did not lie down quietly without kicking, because in future they will think twice before trying to fool me about.

Yesterday morning Phyll sent me a lovely pipe & a box of tobacco. Mrs Cockerill was awfully annoyed at them moving me.

August 5 1918

A few lines to let you know that I'm still at Hayburn Wyke & having quite a decent time. It is not quite so quiet as being all alone at Boundary House. We have now started our daily dips in the sea; of course being so near we can go down in pyjamas with our bathing suits underneath, take a splash in the sea, then come back to the hotel and dress in comfort.

As you know the people here had rather a reputation of making themselves unpleasant, but I have found them quite agreeable & so far they have always obliged when I've asked them for anything. The other evening I went into their sitting room & had quite a long talk with them & the following day when we were having dinner, they sent up to our room by one of the men a huge jug full of cream. The fellows who have been here for some time had quite a shock, this never having happened before, and they put it down to my visit of the previous evening. I must not take all the credit myself, but I think I must inherit this gentle art of telling the tale & being diplomatic under adverse conditions from Father; however, you'll be pleased to hear of the improvement in conditions here.

I'm enclosing a cheque for £5 for Father, another instalment of the loan; by the way, the shoulder of lamb was 8s.4d, carriage 8d, & butter 2s.3d making a total of 11/3; if you want any more let me know. Hoping you are both well.

I Remain, Your Son Jack

317 London Road
Reading
25.8.18

Dear Phyll,

You will notice by the address that I have at last arrived at the R.A.F., just settling down after a most horrible disappointment: no leave & it's all the fault of the people at Scarboro. They heard of the last people getting leave so they kept mine back. A letter follows,

Jack

Nothing more is known of his military career, but a christening mug belonging to Pattie's third son, Thomas Morten Hardman, (Tony), born on 20th October 1918, is inscribed "from Capt. J.C. Morten, his Godfather, in France".

On the other hand, the salver given to JCM and Phyllis Nield on their marriage in February 1925 is inscribed "To Lieutenant J.C. Morten, from his Brother Ex-Officers". Signatories to this are W. Gresty, Harold Breton, Harry Holland, W. Hampson Barratt, F. Grey Burn, Alfred Ward Jones, G.W.F. Franklin, Harry Higgins, T. Edgar Granger, Frank R. Hayes, Reginald J.R. Baker, C.B. Douglas, Marshall Bateman, C.R. Thompson, Gilbert Norbury, and T.P. Wilkinson.

JCM seems convinced that he was gazetted as a Captain, but I cannot find it in the London Gazette. Possibly his wound in France in March 1918 prevented it, or his transfer to the R.A.F.

His Service Record was lost along with many others when the Record Office was bombed in the Second World War.

S.Morten
July 1992

AFTERWARDS

The Memorial to the 7th Manchesters was unveiled at Burlington Street by Colonel Wingate (ex Sirdar in the Sudan and honorary Colonel of the regiment) on Saturday March 22nd 1922. It is now in Whitworth Park , Manchester.

A memorial to the Lacrosse players was unveiled in September 1919.

J.C. Morten married Phyllis Nield on 4th February 1925.

Marshall Bateman married Kathleen Smith on 16th September 1925.

Jack Thorpe became Conservative MP for Rusholme.

Jack Morten died in March 1948, his wife in 1986.

IN GLORIOUS MEMORY
OF ALL RANKS OF THE
7TH · MANCHESTERS
WHO GAVE THEIR LIVES
FOR THEIR COUNTRY
1914 — 1918

7th BATTALION,
THE MANCHESTER REGIMENT,
BURLINGTON STREET, MANCHESTER.

□

Memorial

TO THE

*Officers, Warrant Officers, Non-Commissioned
Officers and Men who fell in the
Great War, 1914-1918.*

□

COMMITTEE:

Lieut.-Colonel J. Newton Brown, D.S.O. *(Chairman).*
Colonel H. Hawkins, V.D.
Lieut.-Colonel H. E. Gresham, T.D.
Major H. G. Davies, T.D.
Major C. Norbury.
Captain R. H. Branthwaite.
Captain J. W. Sutherland.
Lieutenant W. H. Barratt.

---

*The Committee of
The War Memorial Fund of the 7th Battalion, The Manchester Regiment, T.A.,*

request the honour of the Company of

Lt. J. C. Wooden and Lady

at the Unveiling of the Memorial *by*

*General SIR REGINALD F. R. WINGATE, Bart., G.C.B., G.C.V.O.,
G.B.E., K.C.M.G., D.S.O.,
at the Headquarters, Burlington Street, Greenheys, on Saturday, March 25th,
1922, at 2-30 p.m.*

R.S.V.P.
The Secretary,
99 Burlington Street.

Service or Morning Dress.
Medals and Decorations should be worn.

From the Unveiling of the Memorial invitation

7th Battalion, The Manchester Regiment, T.A.

This Battalion was raised as a result of a meeting of Manchester Citizens, held in the Manchester Town Hall on December 1st 1859, the Mayor presiding.

The first title of the Battalion was "The 3rd Regiment of Manchester Volunteers" and the Headquarters were at 75, Bridge Street.

In February 1860, the title was changed to 40th Lancashire Rifle Volunteers.

In September 1880, the title became 16th Lancashire Rifle Volunteers.

In August 1888, the title was again changed to 4th Volunteer Battalion, The Manchester Regiment, as part of the scheme linking the auxiliary forces with the regular regiments.

On the inauguration of the Territorial Force in 1908, the Battalion was designated 7th Battalion, The Manchester Regiment, T. F.

The Headquarters in Burlington Street, having been built and presented to the Battalion by the Earl of Ellesmere, who was in command, were occupied in September 1884.

In 1900-1901, the Battalion furnished voluntary contingents of about 150 Officers and men to the forces engaged in the campaign in South Africa.

The Battalion was mobilised on August 5th 1914, and immediately volunteered for General Service. On September 10th 1914 the Battalion embarked at War strength at Southampton with the 42nd (East Lancs.) Division and proceeded to the Sudan, less one Company, which was divided between Alexandria and Cyprus.

In April 1915, the Battalion rejoined the 42nd Division in Cairo (Egypt), and embarked at Alexandria in the early days of May for Gallipoli, taking part in the operations on the Peninsular, until the Mediterranean Expeditionary Force was withdrawn at the end of 1915.

On arriving in Egypt for the second time, the Battalion was despatched to the Southern Section of the Suez Canal, and was engaged in the operations against the Turks in the Sinai desert until February 1917, when orders were received to proceed to the theatre of war on the western front in Europe. The Battalion embarked at Alexandria, and sailed on March 3rd, disembarking at Marseilles on March 10th 1917. The "Seventh" maintained its individuality throughout the war, and fought continuously until the Armistice was declared.

Second and third line Battalions were raised in 1914-1915.

Casualties during the war numbered several thousands, of whom 902 lost their lives.

Under the reconstituted Territorial Army post-war organisation, the Battalion in 1921 numbered: Officers 25, other Ranks 512, but was ordered to amalgamate with the 6th Battalion in September, and on December 31st 1921 ceased to exist as a separate Unit.

BIBLIOGRAPHY

The Seventh Manchesters, S.J.Wilson, Manchester University Press,   Longmans Green & Co. 1920

With the Manchesters in the East, Manchester University Press, G.B.Hertz 1918

The 42nd East Lancashire Division, London Country Life, Frederick P. Gibbon 1920

Gallipoli, Robert Rhodes James, Batsford 1965

The Recollections of three Manchesters in the Great War, Ed Sue Richardson, N Richardson 1985

Stockport Lads Together, David Kelsall, Stockport MBC, 1989

The Manchester Evening News, 1914 -1918

The Stockport Advertiser, 1914 - 1919

Archive Material in Stalybridge Library

The Manchesters Museum, Ashton Town Hall

The Imperial War Museum

A selection of books from Sigma Leisure

Explore the countryside with Sigma! Find out more about the north-west of England with our super guide books. We have a wide selection of guides to individual towns from Buxton to Lancaster, plus outdoor activities centred on walking and cycling in the great outdoors. Here are some recent highlights:

PEAK DISTRICT DIARY
– Roger Redfern
An evocative book, celebrating the glorious countryside of the Peak District. The book is based on Roger's popular column in *The Guardian* newspaper and is profusely illustrated with stunning photographs. *£6.95*

PUB WALKS SERIES

Sample the delights of country pubs all over England, and enjoy some of the finest walks with our expanding range of 'real ale' books:

☆ PUB WALKS IN THE PEAK DISTRICT
– Les Lumsdon and Martin Smith

☆ MORE PUB WALKS IN THE PEAK DISTRICT
– Les Lumsdon and Martin Smith

☆ PUB WALKS IN LANCASHIRE
– Neil Coates

☆ PUB WALKS IN THE PENNINES
– Les Lumsdon and Colin Speakman

☆ PUB WALKS IN THE LAKE DISTRICT – Neil Coates

☆ PUB WALKS IN THE YORKSHIRE DALES – Clive Price

☆ PUB WALKS IN THE COTSWOLDS
– Laurence Main

☆ PUB WALKS IN OXFORDSHIRE
– Laurence Main

☆ HEREFORDSHIRE WALKS – REAL ALE AND CIDER COUNTRY
– Les Lumsdon

☆ PUB WALKS IN CHESHIRE
– Jen Darling

- all 'Pub Walks' books are just £6.95 each. Many more scheduled in this series – ask for our current list.

There are even more books for outdoor people in our catalogue, including:

☆ EAST CHESHIRE WALKS
– Graham Beech

☆ WEST CHESHIRE WALKS
– Jen Darling

☆ WEST PENNINE WALKS
– Mike Cresswell

☆ NEWARK AND SHERWOOD RAMBLES – Malcolm McKenzie

Even more books from Sigma Leisure . . .

☆ RAMBLES AROUND MANCHESTER
– Mike Cresswell

☆ WESTERN LAKELAND RAMBLES
– Gordon Brown

☆ WELSH WALKS: Dolgellau and the
Cambrian Coast
– Laurence Main and Morag Perrott

☆ WELSH WALKS: Aberystwyth and
District
– Laurence Main and Morag Perrott

☆ OFF-BEAT CYCLING IN THE PEAK
DISTRICT – Clive Smith

☆ 50 BEST CYCLE RIDES IN
CHESHIRE – Graham Beech

*– all of these walking and cycling books are
currently £6.95 each.*

For long-distance walks enthusiasts, we have
several books including:

☆ THE GREATER MANCHESTER
BOUNDARY WALK
– Graham Phythian

☆ THE THIRLMERE WAY
– Tim Cappelli

☆ THE MARCHES WAY
– Les Lumsdon

– all £6.95 each

We also publish:

☆ A guide to the 'Pubs of Old
Lancashire'

☆ Spooky stories about Stockport!

☆ Myths and Legends

– plus many more entertaing and educational
books being regularly added to our list.

All of our books are available from your
local bookshop. In case of difficulty, or to
obtain our complete catalogue, please contact:

Sigma Leisure,
1 South Oak Lane,
Wilmslow, Cheshire SK9 6AR
Phone: 0625 – 531035 Fax: 0625 – 536800

ACCESS and VISA orders welcome – call
our friendly sales staff or use our 24 hour
Answerphone service! Most orders are despatched on the day we receive your order –
you could be enjoying our books in just a
couple of days.

AUTHORS: if you have an interesting
idea for a book, contact us for a
rapid and expert decision. Note that
we are not a 'Vanity Press' – all of our
books earn royalties for their writers.